MW01241761

Pigeon on a Hill

The Power of Faith, Steadfast Support, and a Positive Attitude

Jonathan Stepp

WestBow Press books may be ordered through booksellers or by contacting:

WestBow Press
A Division of Thomas Nelson & Zondervan
1663 Liberty Drive
Bloomington, IN 47403
www.westbowpress.com
1 (866) 928-1240

ISBN: 978-1-4497-8399-0 (sc)
ISBN: 978-1-4497-8398-3 (hc)
ISBN: 978-1-4497-8400-3 (e)

Library of Congress Control Number: 2013902283

Printed in the United States of America.

WestBow Press rev. date: 9/26/2014

CONTENTS

Pigeon on a Hill

Foreword from my Best Friend

What is Pigeon on a Hill? No doubt, it is first and foremost the story of Jonathan's journey battling cancer. But perhaps even more, it is a book of lessons. Lessons in…

Hope, and the power it has to change minds and hearts.
Friendship, and what is means to care for others.
Joy, and the obstacles it can overcome.
Trust, because, after all, the doctors need lots of it.
Faith, and the miracles God can work.

I feel privileged to have played even a small role in the story. The view I was afforded makes me certain that those characteristics are not only true of the book, but that all involved with Jonathan from 2008-2009 felt part of them too. Praise God!

- Owen

HAPPY
17TH
BIRTHDAY
KANSAS
JAYHAWKS

Preface

If you picked up this book, it was for one of two reasons: The first was that you may have heard about me and wanted to support me, but the second is the real reason why I hope you will read through these pages. That reason is that you are human and you will go through hardships in your lifetime. You might not know someone who has cancer or any terminal illness at this point, but I can guarantee that eventually, you will. This is not a story; this is a miracle. I am not a special person, but I was helped and inspired to write this by special people. You might not believe in God, you might not believe in anything, but after reading this account of my journey, it is my prayer that you will believe in hope.

When the going gets rough, it can be difficult to carry on. Nobody knows what tomorrow will bring until it gets here. No one can fully grasp how quickly life can twist and turn, and I am no different. In order to make it through, you have to have faith that things will work out. In addition, it is crucial that you have some sort of support system in place around you. Last, but certainly not least, you have to try and keep a positive outlook on whatever is going on. Anything can go from bad to worse when someone has a poor attitude. I think if I had complained all the time and asked "Why me?" on a daily basis, then I would have been the *true* cancer to everyone surrounding me. Why create more stress or angst when you can just sit back and learn to live with the cards you are dealt? Life gets tough for everyone at some point, and some experience more pain than others. Why? I have come to believe that those who have been given more to handle were born equipped to do just that: be strong and handle it. I had days where I would think I had it bad, and then I would look over at the kid in the room next to mine and see how lucky I was. If you can put things in perspective consistently, this will make everything so much more bearable. I can promise you will enjoy happy times even more, and you will be able to handle sorrow-filled situations more effectively. This is not only for people going through difficult trials in life. This is also for individuals who are the mothers, fathers, children, other family members, or friends who are affected too. If someone gets diagnosed with a disease like cancer, it touches everyone around them. Then in turn it can touch their loved ones. If you are one of those who are dealing with the stress, fear, or uncertainty, please read *this*. Know there is *always* hope. Just like when the sun is behind the clouds, it does not mean it is gone. I have seen it more in a two-year span than ever before. The combination of faith, support, and a positive attitude does not only heal, it changes lives. The following story is about how it changed mine. While there are thousands of stories like this out there, they just don't always get told. I hope you find comfort and joy in the little moments in life. To see these moments makes us appreciate the time we have. It can be a smile, some laughter, a hug, or a hand-written note. I believe everything happens for a reason, and there is a reason I wanted to share about this time in my life. While it has taken me several years to do, I couldn't pass on this opportunity to reach out, because I will truly never know how much or how many people reached out to me. I felt compelled, called, to attempt to be there for those who are where I was. The sad likelihood is that everyone who opens this will be affected directly or indirectly by cancer. This book is for you. And when I say you, I really mean each and *every* one of you.

Introduction

All my life I was healthy. All my life I was raised in a Christian home. Sports were enjoyable and God blessed me with some athletic ability. Amazing how invincible you feel when you have never had a surgery besides getting your teeth pulled.

My two older brothers were healthy, too, and a doctor and a teacher raised me. When I was 17, I was in a cross-country race. The whole season I had waited to run in Lawrence, Kan. at Rim Rock, which is the hardest five-kilometer course of the year.

I set off running at the front of the pack. Would this be the race where I would break into the top seven of my whole team? Since freshman year, I was stuck on JV. I could hear the coaches yell my name and I passed a senior teammate while I was chugging up a hill.

The end of the course was near, and I could see everyone waiting and yelling for his or her respective schools. I started sprinting the last 100 meters on the mud-covered ground and flew past the finish line. This was the fifth time I had raced at Rim Rock, and I felt the same exhaustion set in as I tore my race number off of my running singlet. As I tore the number I felt a sharp sensation on the inside of my right knee. Tendonitis? No, this hurt more and kids had tendonitis all the time. I told my dad about the pain and he suggested that we wait and ice my leg. Little did I know, the pain I felt would not disappear.

It started hurting more in the coming days. When I drove to work I couldn't push the pedal without feeling tension in my leg. Another week passed and I started to limp.

I went on a campout and the weekend was rough because I could not play football, could not run, and could barely even sleep. I would put weight on my knee and feel a prickly sensation. Once I got home I asked if we could set up an appointment with a doctor. It had been several weeks since the knee had started to hurt and I began to think I had done more harm than originally perceived. After a simple x-ray, the doctor told me that often stress fractures don't show up on regular x-rays. He had me lie down and he tried moving my knee into certain positions.

"You need to get an MRI," he said.

A couple of days later I went to have the test done. Forty-five minutes after I finished my MRI we got a phone call.

Dad shared the films with another doctor, and we scheduled a CT scan, a bone scan, and several x-rays. After all those were completed in a two-day period, we received word that something strange had appeared: a cyst. There are two kinds of tumors that develop from a cyst: benign (non-cancerous) and malignant (cancerous).

Hoping for the best, three days later I had an operation to remove a 5-cm. tumor from my tibia at Menorah Medical Center. Dr. Rosenthal placed a ball of putty where he had originally scraped out the tumor and the area around it.

The good news was that the tumor he extracted was small, and he had removed the whole thing. The bad news was what awaited me three days after the surgery. I will never forget what dad told me on that November night.

"Please turn off the TV," he said. "We need to talk about something."

For literally 10 minutes, I was in shock and disbelief. The tumor was not benign, like we originally thought, and I had microscopic cancer cells in my knee.

The next day I met with the orthopedic surgeon, Dr. Rosenthal, and he explained the process that I was about to undertake. Basically, it involved three things: chemotherapy, total knee replacement surgery, and more chemotherapy. I would have treatment done at Children's Mercy Hospital, and the first part would consist of six rounds. After chemotherapy I would have six weeks off in which I would have a metal prosthesis placed in my leg that would extend from my upper shin up to the bottom part of my thigh. I would be on crutches for about eight months. When I was recovered from limb-salvage surgery I would have at least 12 more rounds of chemotherapy, and hopefully at the end of all of this the prognosis would be good.

Osteogenic Sarcoma was the name of my cancer diagnosis. According to cancer.org, around 400 kids under the age of the 20 are diagnosed with this bone cancer each year in the U.S. Bone cancer in teens is more rare, and friends asked me:

"How can you have cancer?"

"What did you do to deserve this?"

"You are only a teenager."

I could only do one thing: pray. *Dear God, please give me strength. Please help me to stay positive. Give my doctors and nurses wisdom and give me courage. Watch over me, I cannot win this fight alone. In Jesus' Name, Amen.*

When I put my life in God's hands that day, it was the most important decision that I have ever made in my life.

I had Osteogenic Sarcoma; Osteogenic Sarcoma did not have me. This was my struggle, this was my fight, but I was *not* fighting alone.

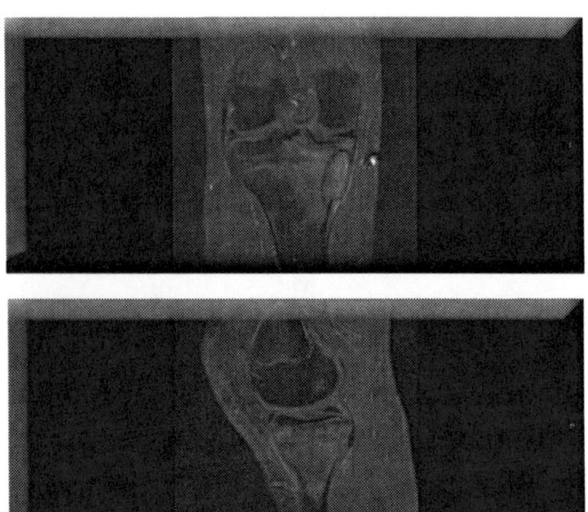

Among the silence, among the shock,
Looking on. I ignore the clock.
My life is now a piece of glass,
Fragile, gentle, falling fast.
My future, months confined in space
My challenge.

I shut my eyes to shut out day,
To Christ my Lord I humbly pray:
My life is yours; Your will my command.
Please save me and extend Your hand.
That is when the silence broke
For in the air a word He spoke.

My fear was shattered there and then
I knew salvation conquered sin
At that moment from Heaven came a sound,
That sound was Hope.
God's grace was found

Chapter 1: Attitude

Dedicated to: Matt Wassom, Clinical Psychologist at Children's Mercy

In the first five minutes after being diagnosed with Osteogenic Sarcoma, I made a choice. My choice was to make this fight with cancer the most positive situation it could be. Even though I had made that decision, it was not something I could carry out on my own. While getting treated at Children's Mercy Hospital, I met a child psychologist named Matt. He would visit me during the rounds of chemotherapy, and he was a positive influence in my life. We could talk about anything going on, but mostly, he made me feel comfortable in my new setting. To be honest, I mainly talked with him about sports. Yet he was calming, collected, and friendly. Those were only some of the characteristics he possessed. To me, keeping a positive outlook was the best way to go. Matt was always there if I needed to talk, and part of what made treatments do-able was his help throughout the process.

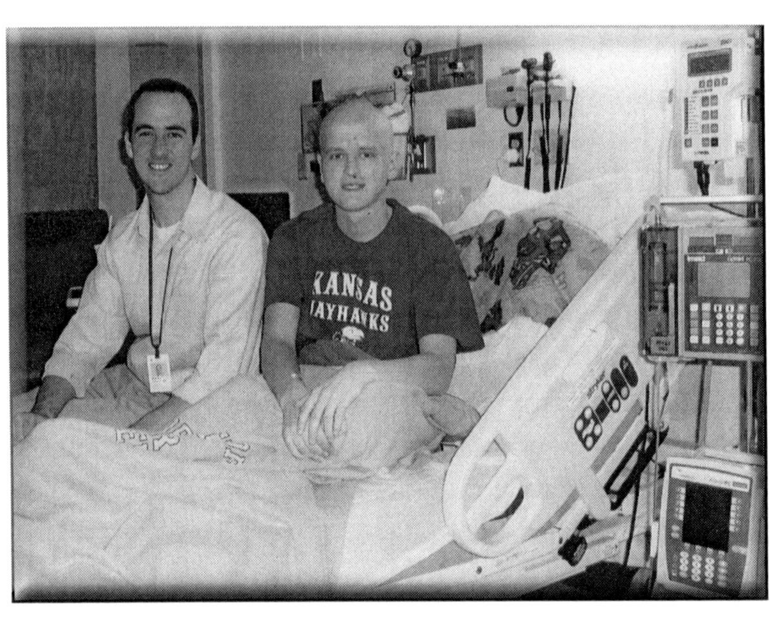
KANSAS

Attitude

How does your attitude affect people? It makes all the difference in the world! Throughout this struggle with cancer, there were times where I felt like giving up. Who knows what a difference there was in the first five minutes after hearing the diagnosis? God told me that I would be all right and I listened to Him.

Before starting the whole process, we went to California to visit my brother and to celebrate Thanksgiving with my family. This was the last time that I would be outside of Kansas City for a year. Fitting enough was the fact that I was there over Thanksgiving. My family and I arrived in San Jose and met my brother at Santa Clara University, the beautiful resort they call a college. Giant trees, gorgeous flowers, vast ocean and beautiful blue sky surround the campus in each direction.

As my parents pushed me in a wheelchair through the beautiful Spanish architecture of the college, I began to think about how my friends and family would cope with the news that I had cancer. I didn't know what they would say, but I knew people would be worried. My parents were doing all right with the news because I was. That was when I realized what to do to "calm the storm." *You've got to believe that you can beat this. You have to believe that you will be OK.* For my sanity, I had to be strong. Seventy-five percent of the outcome is how you deal with the process. Sometimes it's not the cancer that's the disease; it is your bad attitude. Maintaining a positive outlook not only helps you, it benefits those around you as well.

When people hear the word "cancer" they make assumptions. They wonder when I will lose my hair and energy. When will I start radiation? Luckily I didn't have to undergo that process, because my cancer isn't treated with radiation.

The hardest part of cancer is the lingering feeling. You are constantly reminded that you have it, so you come to grips with it and you get used to it. You don't perk your ears up every time someone uses the word anymore. That's just the nature of the beast: people will talk about your situation. You are desensitized pretty quickly though, and it comes up in regular conversation. Before I had cancer, I really had no interest in the medical field whatsoever. My dad is a neurosurgeon and I thought I would never enjoy being around other sick people. But things change when your life takes a turn that you don't anticipate.

Thanksgiving dinner at Stokes Adobe, one of my favorite restaurants (only been there twice, so the fact it's one of my favorites tells you something) really put things into perspective. Football did not matter, and though the food was excellent, it did not really matter either. I thanked God that I was still alive and that I was with people I loved. People are what matter the most in everyday life, not material possessions. Relationships with friends and family would be what would get me through the next year of treatment and surgery. I would need lots of help and lots of love, and that is just what God gave me. I looked around the table at my two brothers, Samuel and Nathan, and my parents, Tim and Debbie, and I felt blessed to know I had a loving family.

Growing up in a Christian home and trying to live my life based on Christian values provided me with a very sturdy foundation. Family that loved and cared for me is one of the things that I took for granted. I tried my hardest to treat everyone I met on my journey with kindness and respect, because that is what I desired in return. It is amazing how a little thing like a smile can affect someone. In my opinion, listening is so much more important than talking. Up to this point in my life I would ask God to help me and then I would not always be eager to listen. When I talk to anyone, one of the whole goals of conversation is to learn about what is going on in their life, not my own.

God is so good that even at the sunrise stage of my cancer, he gave me the wisdom to know that if I trusted in Him, anything was possible. *"I can do all things through Him who strengthens me."* – Philippians 4:13

Time in California helped me get my mind off treatment, and the weather was nearly perfect throughout our stay. Kansas City, however, was just starting to get freezing cold. It is funny how much weather can affect people's moods. Before the holidays everyone loves seeing snow and putting up their Christmas trees. After Christmas many people say that they want to jump right into spring. It had a big effect on me because crutches don't bode well on wet and slippery surfaces.

A couple of days after I had arrived back in Kansas City, my parents and I headed downtown to Children's Mercy Hospital. I would be receiving all 18 rounds of chemotherapy there on the 4 Henson Hematology/Oncology floor. That day I met my oncologist, Dr. Richard Shore, and my primary nurse, Nancy Terwilliger. At first, I was a little nervous because I was in a brand new environment, but the people that calmed my nerves were the care assistants: Jamie, Shelley, David, and Kaylynne. That day I was introduced to each of them, and they would become my friends.

Jamie had graduated from a high school close to mine and was a big KU fan. She was petite, but she had a huge heart and I could always joke around with her.

Shelley was very good friends with Jamie and she was taller than I am! Whenever I needed anything to eat or drink or really just someone to chat with, I could depend on one of these nice people to deliver.

Kaylynne was also a Jayhawk fan and she had always wanted to be a nurse. She started nursing school this same year.

David is one of the main people who inspired me to write a book. He was very interested in martial arts as well as becoming a full-fledged author. He had published a beautiful anthology of poetry and was working on a six-novel series. I will never forget something he said to me: “You don’t have to have special ability to write, you just have to have a passion for doing it.”

Dr. Shore was a friendly, balding man. He had an East-coast accent and a beard that reminded me of Richard Dreyfuss in “Mr. Holland’s Opus.” When I talked to him for the first time he let me know three things. The first was that I would spend a lot of time in the hospital over the next year. The second thing he told me was that although it is one of the hardest regimens of chemotherapy, I would get through it OK; it would just take time. Last but not least, he said that while at Children’s Mercy, he, Nancy, the nurses, and the doctors were all working on the same team to help me beat Osteogenic Sarcoma. At that moment God touched my heart and reiterated the fact that as long as I trusted in Him, everything would be OK.

That same day, on our way to my last dinner before the start of treatment, someone texted me the lyrics to a song by Rascal Flatts called “Skin.” The song is about a girl named Sarabeth who gets diagnosed with cancer.

There are three parts of that song that I love. The first part is "But we're gonna take care of you." I knew that the nurses and doctors were going to take care of me because God is in total control. You have to put your trust in God, because with Him you have a base as sturdy as a rock. Every day when I woke up, I told myself that one day I would be cancer-free.

The second part that I like is "I think we caught it in time." Luckily for me, I am around today to tell my story. I am a survivor in large part because of the attitude God gave me to approach the whole situation with. *I am going to live my life for Christ and let His light shine through my heart. I am going to try to set an example by being strong and putting my life in His hands.* A lot of people want to know God, but when it comes time to commit their life to Him, they get cold feet. They think: *I can take care of myself; I don't really need God, do I?* The only way God is going to do things in your life is if you let Him come into your heart and honor Him in what you do. Live your life with the attitude that you cannot live without his Holy grace.

The final part that stood out to me was, "And for a moment, she isn't scared." Cancer is frightening to people because it is unpredictable. When I got diagnosed with cancer, I instantly told God that I wanted His help. I did not want to be living in fear constantly. He truly took all my fears and He got rid of them. Other than the potential of recurrence, I am not truly afraid of much of anything after this experience. There is no reason for me to be afraid. Everything in my life is run according to God's plan, and the worries that I had in life before I had cancer seem petty now.

Chapter 2: Blessings

Dedicated to: My mom, Debbie

Each time I talk to my mom, she always tries to look at everything in a positive light, because she is a very positive person.

Although I missed a whole semester of school, I was not in the hospital during any major holidays or for my birthday. That was a blessing. I had only been to the Emergency Room three times. I consider that a blessing, too. I had the opportunity to get back to a normal life before the start of my senior year in high school. I would be with all of my friends on a day-to-day basis. In the past that is something I always took for granted. How I was able to graduate on time will always be a mystery to me, but it became a reality because of the help and encouragement I received. My mom is someone that can always cheer me up and make me feel better, because she can always make me smile. A mother's love is just different, because she brought me into this world. She cares about my brothers and me more than anything, and she would do whatever it takes to make me feel better. Her life is a blessing to me, and her love is one of the most valuable possessions I could ever have!

KANSAS
PERIOD
ARIZONA
KU
KANSAS
15

Blessings

Lucky. That is a word that describes those last ten months of my life. I still can barely grasp how blessed I am. The small size of my tumor was extremely rare and extremely fortunate. God also provided me with the opportunity of having one of the best children's hospitals in the country twenty minutes away from my house (fifteen if we were speeding). When you are scheduled to spend ten months somewhere for treatment, you want to feel at home. Before I went to Children's Mercy in downtown Kansas City, Mo., I knew one person there, a patient who happens to be someone who I look up to a lot. Now I know over 150 people, all of whom I consider friends or at the very least, blessings in my life. Although I know some better than others, I consider them all part of another family.

December 5 rolled around, and it was the day before I had my surgery to install a double-sided port-a-cath in my upper chest (just below the collarbone) to make chemotherapy easier and more comfortable. My mental state was: *You are going to beat this cancer because God is watching over you.* One of the first blessings of my journey was the fact that I was starting treatment at one of the happiest times of the year. Christmas was twenty days away and my doctor jokingly told me that this would be the year to "milk Christmas for all it's worth." I was excited for the holidays and most of the day I tried to pray and enjoy my last day of school for the foreseeable future.

From the moment I got home I was on the phone. People were calling me and talking to me and encouraging me. I probably got over 100 texts that day from people that knew what I was about to begin treatment. By that point a great number of my friends knew about the cancer and they had contacted me to let me know that they loved me. I did not feel like I was doing anything special, I felt like I was doing what God wanted me to do.

That night, I got a text message from a friend in my youth group that I still remember even if it's been long since deleted from my phone. It said: "Hey just wanted to tell you that I am praying for you and that I hope everything goes well tomorrow. Know that I love you, and you're one of my best friends" – 10:27 p.m. 12/05/07

I kept the message because it gave me hope and I also kept it to remind me how blessed I am when it comes to my friends. Throughout this process I kept every letter of support that I have ever gotten in a wicker box in my room. The Lord has given me such a great support system and I can't thank everyone enough for what they have done for me.

In order to receive chemotherapy and get blood counts checked without having to poke a vein every time, they insert a port-a-cath. They would need to make a small incision on the right side of my upper chest (around my heart and above my ribs) to insert a double-sided port. The catheter of the port extends into one of the central veins. It is a drum-shaped device accessed by a needle to give chemotherapy. The operation would take 60 minutes. I got into the bed and they inserted an IV into my right arm and then the anesthesiologist came in.

"I am going to give you some medicine that will make you fall asleep for a couple of hours. It might sting going in but it won't hurt for very long," he said with a wink and a smile that had likely been lighting up kids' faces for years.

He was right, it stung for about 10 seconds and while it was administered I said a prayer. *Dear God, please help my surgery to go well and please help it to not be painful. I thank you for this only being my second surgery I have ever had. Please give me strength and courage. In Your Name, Amen.*

The next thing I knew, I was being pushed down the hall and my parents told me they would see me when I woke up. The doctors were asking me if I felt sleepy and I nodded my head. We got to the Operating Room and they slid me onto the table. The doctors offered me a blanket and then had me take a couple of deep breaths in a mask. And then…

I opened my eyes and I wasn't in the O.R. I saw my mom and dad next to my bed and I asked, "Where am I?"

"Floor 4 Henson," they replied.

The left side of my chest was hurting badly and I let out a deep painful sigh. My dad told me I was hooked up to a morphine pump. It gave me a certain amount of pain medicine in an hour but it also had a little button I could push that would give me a little bit extra if I was really hurting. I felt very tired and I started to itch quite a bit. We rang the "nurse call button" and 20 seconds later a tall, blond nurse named Tiffany walked into my room and asked if I needed something. I told her I was itching and she sympathetically told me it was probably from the morphine. She ran and got some medicine and inserted it into my IV line. Gradually, the itching sensations subsided. Unfortunately, after I got the medicine I started getting hot. Sweating was a side effect of the medicine used to stop the itching. At the same time, I was starting to feel slightly nauseous. I fell asleep and woke up several times throughout the night and then got back to sleep. While I was asleep, apparently they had been giving me a medicine called Zofran through my IV. My nurse the next day, R.J., came in and gave me a dose. R.J. was a tall nurse with a crew-cut and glasses. He was built like a football player but he had a very kind voice that made me feel very secure.

"Can I get you anything, bud? Is the pain going down?"

I told him I was doing OK and he said to let him know if he could get me anything.

I nodded and he closed my door. When I look back, I always took my parents staying with me for granted. I must have thought: *Everyone's parents are here, right?* Wrong. Sadly, there were patients that were alone most of the time. I was in Room 2, and there were 24 other rooms on 4-H.

Later in the day my best friend, Owen Gray, called me to see if I wanted some company.

Not many people that I know are as nice as this kid. He would do anything for me if he had to, and I would do the same for him. He had been my best friend since second grade. We shared the love of sports, especially football. Owen is over 6'3" and is about 220 pounds. He could never hurt anyone, though, and so he decided he would not play.

That night Owen visited me in my room. He brought some sports magazines with him. He wasn't scared about what I was about to face because he believed me when I told him I wasn't scared. He had been one of the first people I told about what was going on.

Owen and I talked for a couple of hours and then he headed home. God reminded me that night what a blessing it was to have Owen as my friend. He is so loyal and such an inspiration to me as a person.

I fell asleep and when I woke up not too long afterwards, my stomach felt terrible. I threw up. My night nurse, Amy, was called in and she gave some Zofran.

"I'm sorry that you threw up!" she said. "That morphine is no fun."

Shortly I fell back asleep and I felt a lot better. However, the feeling of someone prodding my chest with a stethoscope awakened me. A nurse about my height with long blond hair and turquoise scrubs was checking my breathing.

"Hi, I'm Mandy and I'll be your nurse today."

"I'm Jonathan, it is nice to meet you."

"Nice to meet you too," she said with a smile.

My doctor visited me and told me that today I was starting chemotherapy. He told me that it might make me nauseous so they were scheduling out Zofran every six hours to help my stomach and control nausea. The chemotherapy agent that they would be using for round one of treatment was called Cisplatin. Known for causing fatigue, hair loss, hearing loss, low blood platelets, low red and white cell counts, and extreme nausea, this would be the worst kind of chemo that I would get because they gave it with another kind of chemo called Doxorubicin. Some of the side effects of "Dox," as they called it, are hair loss, sensitivity to the sun, possible loss of fertility, heart damage, and fever and chills. I would only get this duo four times throughout the course of 18 rounds, and I soon figured out why.

Mandy came into my room and she was wearing a mask with purple protective gloves and a yellow protective gown over her scrubs. She hung a bag of clear liquid (Cisplatin) and a bag of "Kool-Aid" (Doxorubicin is a red liquid) on my IV pole. *All right cancer, I am ready for you. My boxing gloves are on, and I don't care if it takes 18 rounds. God is going to beat you.*

Cisplatin requires eight hours of pre-hydration and Doxorubicin requires only a couple before you can receive it. Mandy spiked the chemo, un-clamped the roller that allowed the liquid to fill the measuring cylinder, and set each chemo drug to run at a certain pace over a certain amount of time.

And so it began. Three hours passed and I did not have any nausea! *Well, this isn't so bad,* I thought. The Cisplatin was a six-hour infusion that you got twice in one round, and the Dox ran over a period of 48 hours. Mandy came in because my IV started beeping (a sound that I would hear countless times over the course of the next ten months). She reset the chemo rate and administered more Zofran through my line, and suddenly my stomach lurched. I grabbed a bin and vomited. Mandy grabbed me a towel, and after I was through she asked if I was OK. My face was covered in sweat and I told her I was very nauseous.

"I am going to try a drug called Ativan," she said.

She left and came back a few minutes later. Twenty minutes after she had given me the Ativan, I started to feel jittery. I looked around my room and felt dizzy. I started to space out and I became antsy to the point that I thought I should get up and jump around. I could not lie still so I probably looked like I was having a seizure. The walls looked like they were moving, and I took this as a bad sign. My parents asked how I felt and I reached for the bin but couldn't find it in time. I puked all over my sheets while they called in Mandy. She held the bin under my mouth until I stopped throwing up. Immediately Mandy brought in clean sheets and she and a care assistant changed my bed while I sat in a chair, still jittery, and changed my shirt.

I got back into bed and Mandy asked, "Do you need anything else? Do you want a cold washcloth for your head?"

Mandy walked out into the hall and the next thing I knew she had put a wet washcloth on my forehead. I thanked her and she smiled and walked out. I thought about my chemotherapy and I imagined God saying: *Why are you dwelling on your treatment? I will take care of you.*

Having heard these words in my head I tried to relax and read my magazines. I was reading *Sports Illustrated* and Mandy noticed when she came back in to reset my chemo. She asked me about sports, and when we started talking (even though my stomach felt bad), I noticed that Mandy and I had created a bond. She was my nurse throughout the remainder of my hospital stay, and I knew that she was an answer to my prayer.

During my first round, I probably threw up more in five days then I had in my entire life. The chemo infusion had finished a couple of days earlier but I was not allowed to go home until I could keep food and water down. *Dear God, please help me to feel better. Thank you for all the blessings that you have given me.*

It is amazing how tired you get when you throw up. After about five days in the hospital I finally stopped puking and tried eating crackers. I sipped on juice and I was weaker than I have ever been in my whole life. *My entire life I have been healthy, so this is going to be an adjustment, but I can handle it.*

The doctors came around on morning rounds and told me that I could go home. Mandy then said she would de-access my port.

"Now don't come back here for a while, OK?" she joked with me.

My care assistant took us down to the parking lot. We then drove home and I was very glad to see my dog, Dylan. Dylan was a rescue dog that we got at the end of my fourth grade year. He was a mutt, but he is one of the cutest dogs on Earth. He has a Maltese face, Westie fur (white with champagne-colored blotches strewn across it), and a Poodle tail that is very whip-like and fluffy.

I was on crutches and I really wanted to take a shower. Before I did, however, I thought it would be OK to eat. I had some more juice and then made the ill-advised decision to munch on a peanut butter and cheese sandwich. I ate it and then took my shower. As soon as I stood up on my left leg in the tub, I turned on the water and started washing. Little did I know that due to my chemo, when I was finished, I could barely get on to my toilet (right next to my shower) without feeling like I would faint. I called my mom and she helped me dry off. She then grabbed my clothes and I was sweating just putting them on.

Immediately after collapsing on my bed, I got underneath the covers and fell asleep saying a prayer. In the middle of the night I woke up hot and nauseated, and started to vomit. We tried putting the dissolvable Zofran on my tongue, but it is of no use when you have already started throwing up. It was then we realized that the purple pill would not be the solution to the nausea problems.

The next day my parents drove me to the clinic and I couldn't stop throwing up in the car on the way there. They ran fluids over a course of six hours and I took a much-needed nap. At some point Dr. Shore came in with and told me, "This is most likely the worst you will ever feel. Next treatment we will try the other non-drowsy anti-emetic. Like I say to my patients, chemotherapy is very do-able, but getting through stages like this is the toughest part."

On the 15 minute route to get back to my house, I realized how blessed I was to get the first round out of the way. The result was that Cisplatin/Doxorubicin kicked my butt and I felt more fatigued than ever. Even though I was tired and only a week ago my weight was 150 lbs. (now at 135.5), I clung to a bible verse: *"Come to me, all you who are weary and burdened and I will give you rest."* - Matthew 11:28

That verse encouraged me to accept that I would be tired a lot, but that it was going to be OK. Even though this was just the beginning of the fight, I knew that if God was at the center of this and if I put my trust in Him, I could handle a lot.

Chapter 3: Courage

Dedicated to: Kevin Everett

Injury is a part of life in the National Football League. But being told that you may never be able to walk again after a severe spinal cord injury is entirely different. Kevin Everett, a former tight end for the Buffalo Bills, suffered a vicious hit during a game on September 9, 2007. Some doctors thought the injury could be life threatening, and at the very least they thought Kevin might be paralyzed. After undergoing surgery and periods of waiting and uncertainty, Kevin persevered, completed extensive physical therapy and got to the point where he could walk again. He might not have the opportunity to play football anymore, but he has touched the hearts of thousands with his determination and bravery. He kept his chin up and worked hard, and his courage gave me strength.

Courage

You know what is truly amazing? How much inspiration you can get when friends, family, and people you don't even know send you cards. It was the holiday season, after all, and what better way to show that people cared than by sending nice notes.

Hi Jonathan,

We spoke with your dad at church yesterday, and we heard that you are enduring some very difficult treatment.

We hope it is at least a small comfort to know you are surrounded by the love and prayers of many friends... We are two of those friends. We will continue to hold you in our prayers and wait for good news.

With friends' help,
Dick & Mary Ann Olson

Debbie, Tim, Jonathan, Nathan, and Samuel,

We were so very sorry to hear about Jonathan's illness. Certainly this will be a painful and difficult time for you all, but we are hopeful that this treatment is successful and we will all soon be celebrating his full recovery.

If there is anything we can do to make things easier for you, please let us know. In the meantime, you are very much in our thoughts.

Best wishes,
Barb, Chuck, Amanda & Taylor Haviland

My friends sent me "get well" cards and gifts. People would say encouraging words that made me feel like I could face anything if I could make it through having cancer. In my opinion, courage lives in everyone's hearts, it's whether they recognize it and have the strength to use it that counts. Anyone can have courage, and it especially helps to have the support of your loved ones.

My mom is a great cook but she wouldn't really have as much time to make me home-cooked meals in the upcoming months. No worries. There were plenty of nice people that would prepare food for our family. When we got home my pastor, Dr. Heather Entrekin, had dropped off homemade bread, beef stew, and buttery chocolate chip cookies. One of my cross country coaches, Mr. Pennington, brought over chicken noodle soup and vegetables made by his wife. By the time my first week out of the hospital was ending, our refrigerator was overflowing with food, and so was our freezer.

People's generosity was astounding, and once I could actually enjoy it, the food that we had received was excellent. Staying at home during the winter is not an easy thing to do. I was awaiting my next round of chemo, which would supposedly be easier to get through.

During that first week home Owen visited me and we talked about how school was going. He said everyone missed me and it was not quite the same without me. Mr. Pennington came over one night and we talked about what I was experiencing. He brought gag gifts with him, including a plastic Nerf gun (to "shoot my dog or future tutors with," he joked), club soda (to help with nausea), and a book written about faith and sports by Tony Dungy, who was the head coach of the Indianapolis Colts at the time. Having that meeting and knowing that he cared enough to show his support meant a great deal to me.

I knew that cancer could slow me down, but I started to realize that it could not stop me from being who I was. Final exams were coming up, and I didn't have time to feel tired. *I have to study. Overcome your energy-loss by supplementing your time and using it wisely.* And that is exactly what I tried to do.

The week before Christmas was the week of finals. I missed the first day of exams but luckily you only have to take your first hour exam that day anyway. On Wednesday I went to see Coach Hair for my Team Games' final.

"Jonathan, you don't need to take the final," he said. "I can write you a pass somewhere else if you need to study."

He wrote me a pass to Painting so I could make up the final. *What a blessing.* Coach Hair told me good luck and that I was "one brave kid."

I crutched on down to the art wing and saw Ms. Schnakenberg. Luckily her second hour was testing so I took my final with them. After 90 minutes I had completed the test and I headed home.

The next day I had my French final, and I was not well prepared. My friend Alexa Schnieders, however, was in French 2 and getting ready to switch into French 3 because she was so good at it. She met with me and helped me study. This act of kindness directly impacted how I did on the test, because I was better prepared.

The next day I went in and took the test for French. I wasn't worried and I even finished early. That day I also took my choir test, which involved placing the sharps and flats on the scale. We had taken the same final every year for each semester. Students volunteered to grade it in class, and I found out that I had received an A. Mr. Resseguie gave me a bear hug and wished me good luck.

I went home that night and studied for my World History and English finals. My energy was very low even though the blood counts were coming up. I looked outside into the dark winter night and thought about where I would be during all of second semester. I would not be with my friends at school, but with nurses at the hospital. I would have one teacher for English and World History, and another teacher for math who would come to our house for an hour every week. *The cancer cells in my body don't care if I have time to adjust to a new lifestyle, so I just need to do it.* I fell asleep reading over my English notes and the next thing I knew my mom was in waking me up.

The World History final was not easy but I had studied long enough that I recalled most of the material. I finished the final right before the bell rang and my teacher, Mr. Ricker, shook my hand and said, "Good luck."

Last but not least I had to take my English final. This was the final that I was a little bit nervous for because the review packet (even though it was for extra credit) was pretty big! I could not believe the first semester of my junior year was coming to a close… *Look how fast this school year is going by. Your chemo treatments will probably seem long, but before you know it you will be finished with them.* The test was thankfully not as hard as the review packet led me to believe, but it still took the full 90 minutes to complete. Like several other teachers, Ms. Gehring wished me good luck and gave me a hug.

As I got off the elevator and slowly crutched out of the office entrance, I came to grips with the fact that this might be the last time that I would be at Shawnee Mission East for a while. Although it felt good to be finished with school for the semester, I was definitely behind on Christmas shopping. I only had a few days to shop, so when the opportunity came to go with my brother Sam and his friend Mike, I jumped.

Sam is the older of my two brothers, a highly intelligent, highly social student (who was 23 at the time). We were out and about for a couple of hours and then we headed home to find that my dad had carried our artificial Christmas tree upstairs and placed it in our dining room. I was so excited, even in the midst of my upcoming chemo treatments.

This was one of the best days I had during the last ten months. Everyone was so happy, everyone was together, and I remember saying to my Aunt Amy, "This Christmas is very special, but next Christmas will be one of the greatest I will ever have."

What a blessing that I get to be out of the hospital for Christmas Day. The evening meant a lot to me because of the fellowship and love that our family shared.

The next morning, I expected us to open our stockings followed by our presents, at the traditional 9:00 or 9:30 time window. By the time we all got up, however, it was 1:00 in the afternoon. This was by far the latest that we had ever started our Christmas festivities.

We were about to open our stockings when, all of a sudden, my dog, Dylan ripped a present out of his. None of us could stop laughing for about five straight minutes. Wrapping paper was all over the ground when we finished, so we picked it up before we headed from the family room to the dining room.

A wide array of magnificent color highlighted our Christmas tree. From the ornaments down to the gifts it was a sight to behold. My parents had asked me what I wanted for Christmas earlier in the week, and the present only God could give me tugged on their hearts. "All I want is to get well."

"We are working on that, but is there anything in particular you want?"

I ended up not answering that question and when we were down to the last present, my parents told us to open it together.

One…two…three! We ripped the paper off faster than you can say "Merry Christmas." Excitement was beaming. A Nintendo Wii! Wow. How did they find one? It seemed like they were sold out almost everywhere. At that moment I thought about what I loved the most during Christmas: giving. When you give a gift, people get excited. When you know you gave them something that they really wanted, you are overcome by joy. Who in the history of all time was the greatest giver? Jesus Christ, because he took away our sins when he died on the cross so that we could live with God for eternity in Heaven.

When I thought about my upcoming treatments, the word "Savior" came to mind.

I read somewhere that when Jesus is in your life, cancer becomes so limited that:

It cannot cripple your love,
It cannot shatter your hope,
It cannot corrode your faith,
It cannot destroy peace,

It cannot kill friendship,
It cannot suppress your memories,
It cannot silence your courage,
It cannot invade your soul,
It cannot steal eternal life,
And it cannot conquer the spirit.

Christmas honors the day that our Savior was born, and without His birth, we would all perish.

"It is God who arms me with strength and makes my way perfect. He makes my feet like the feet of a deer; he enables me to stand on the heights. He trains my hands for battle; my arms can bend a bow of bronze. You give me your shield of victory, and your right hand sustains me; you stoop down to make me great. You broaden the path beneath me, so that my ankles do not turn. I pursued my enemies and overtook them; I did not turn back till they were destroyed. I crushed them so that they could not rise; they fell beneath my feet. You armed me with strength for battle; you made my adversaries bow at my feet. You made my enemies turn their backs in flight, and I destroyed my foes." – Psalm 18:32-40

That verse gives me courage. When I think that things look gloomy, I remember what Jesus faced. He was whipped 39 times and then forced to carry a heavy wooden cross up a hill. Eventually, His hands and feet were nailed to that cross. In the face of adversity, I was inspired when I thought about His sacrifice. I knew I could conquer my cancer because God was going to get me through it. I was not alone.

Chapter 4: Doctors

Dedicated to: My dad, Tim

Four simple words hit him harder than a freight train: "Your son has cancer." My dad tries to take care of sick people every day, but he never knew that he would end up taking care of me for a total of nine months straight. He felt so sad when he told me that the tumor removed from my knee was malignant, because he deals with cancer patients on a frequent basis. Both of my grandfathers died of cancer, and one of my grandmothers would later die of cancer as well. I have had lots of doctors take care of me during this process, but none of them have been more comforting than my dad. He was honest with me about everything, even when the going got tough, and that is something that means a great deal to me. I love you so much, dad, and I am so thankful that I have you as my father.

ARIZONA
PERIOD
EXIT
KANSAS
15

Doctors

Christmas Day had come and gone, and I had the December 26 off. The next day after I would start the second round of chemotherapy. Winter is generally not as enjoyable after Christmas because you have about a week left before your break is over. It didn't matter for me this year.

The day after Christmas I was playing video games when I heard the doorbell ring. I was delighted to find two of my good friends, Tucker Nelson and Ali Fisher, walking down the stairs into the basement. What they were holding in their hands was truly unbelievable. Each of them had a box filled to the brim with different kinds of caps. They told me that they had gone to our former elementary school and asked teachers to donate them. Tucker and Ali both made phone calls and emailed a large amount of people that they knew in order to get all of these. There were all types, shapes, colors, sizes, and styles. NASCAR hats, golf tournament hats, baseball caps, etc. I was speechless when they placed the boxes beside me. *They found all these hats to use so that I could cover my balding head.*

"We figured that you would want a different hat for every day of your chemo treatment," Tucker said. "My dad's friend is sending more sometime soon!"

In all, there were probably around 150 hats in the cardboard boxes. I gave both of them hugs and said I hoped I would see them soon.

Later that night I was taking a shower to get ready to go to dinner with one of my good friends, Paige Anderson, and something strange happened. As I was washing my hair, part of it came out. I felt the spot where I had pulled, and where there used to be hair there was now just soft, sensitive skin. *This is not a great time for my hair to be falling out.* I started to pull more, but then realized that this would take a lot longer than expected. I turned off the shower. I looked in the mirror and about half of it was still left. I called Paige and I told her I would need another 30 minutes to get ready. I probably spent a total of an hour in the shower pulling it all out. Paige was very patient and supportive, as were her parents.

The next day I woke up around 7:45 to get ready to commute to the hospital. My mom put the cream on the port to numb it (it always took about 30 minutes to numb) and we headed over to Children's Mercy. I arrived in the clinic, where I was amazed the receptionist remembered my name.

There was only one other family waiting in the clinic and it only took about five minutes for Jamie to come out and call my name. She led us to the back where there were several kids waiting with their families. A couple of kids were getting blood transfusions and some were being pre-hydrated for chemotherapy.

As the nurse, Mary, started to wipe off the cream and wash my port, she asked me what my favorite Christmas gift was.

"My brothers and I got a Wii so we were pretty excited," I said.

We were all amused when she replied, "I've played the Wii with my kids!"

Mary had a way of making me feel like everything was going to be OK because she had a warm smile on her face every time she laughed. It just lit me up!

"Jonathan, Dr. Shore said that we were going to try Kytril during this admission because the Zofran didn't work very well for you," she said.

"Could you also make sure that he doesn't receive Ativan anymore, please? It made him very antsy and he felt really out of it," my dad said.

To be honest, I don't really know what I would have done if my dad was not with me. Being a doctor, he was familiar with the medicines that I received and he spoke the medical jargon physicians communicate with.

The curtain opened. Dr. Shore and Nancy walked into our infusion area.

"You look a little better than the last time I saw you," he said. "How do you feel?"

"I feel a lot better, thanks," I told him. "Does the Kytril usually work pretty well for nausea?"

"The hardest group of cancer patients to find an effective anti-nausea regimen for is teenage boys," he explained. "You are growing and your body chemistries change so much in a matter of months. The Kytril works for a lot of patients, but it doesn't necessarily work for everyone."

God, please help the Kytril to control my nausea. I know the nurses and doctors will do everything they can to help me get through this round without any discomfort.

Nancy took me to an exam room and gave me a check-up. I would get used to this very quickly.

"Everything looks good, now we are just waiting to make sure your blood counts are high enough," she said with a smile.

Several hours passed and we still didn't have a room. A red-haired nurse named Rochelle gave me a sheet of paper with all of my blood chemistries on it. To receive Methotrexate, your red blood count (hemoglobin), white blood count, blood platelets, and the pH of your urine have to be at a certain level.

"All of your counts are in the normal range but we still don't have a room on the floor yet," she said. "We're running a pretty full ship today."

Patience isn't a virtue when you have cancer — it is a necessity. A huge part of the 10-month process was the waiting involved. Waiting for lab results to come back, waiting for energy, waiting for nausea to go away, and waiting for healing... This waiting process could take seconds, it could take minutes, or it could take hours, mornings, afternoons, evenings, days, nights, weekends, weeks, or months. God showed me that I would need patience to get through this process, and I trusted in Him. *The only one who knows what the outcome of this process will be is God.*

Mary came up to me and said, "Well Jonathan, the good news is that we have a room, the bad news is that it is 4:00!"

A huge blessing that God bestowed on me was making time go by quickly when I wanted it to. I had already been at Children's Mercy since 8:30 and it was now almost 4. *Have I really been here for seven and a half hours? It certainly didn't feel that long.*

Typically I would always ask for water and that is what my care assistant, Stacie, brought me. She checked vital signs (blood pressure & temperature), which was probably done 500 times throughout my tenure at Children's Mercy. In order to receive Methotrexate, the pH of my urine had to be in between a certain range. The waiting process involved with this particular kind of chemo would prove to be the most taxing because I would do it 12 different times.

About an hour before I was scheduled to start receiving Methotrexate I was given an IV dose of Kytril by my nurse, Kara. Kara had curly dark hair and always wore a big smile on her face.

Kara brought the chemo after the Kytril set in and it was a neon yellow color. With Methotrexate, they give you two bags of it that each run for about two to three hours. They pump you with so much fluid (six hours of pre-hydration) that on the first night your C.A. wakes you up every two hours to go to the bathroom and excrete it.

“This will run for three hours and then I’ll put up another bag of it,” Kara explained. “After the second bag is finished, we will give you more and more fluid so you can flush it out. Some kids get their Methotrexate levels to .01 or below in two to three days, and some kids excrete the chemo a lot slower. Hopefully you will be faster so you can go home soon,” Kara said.

Out of the chemo drugs I would receive, the one that takes the most pro-activity is Methotrexate. You have to drink water constantly and get rid of it before you go home. It also causes you to get a little puffy because your fluid intake is so great.

Surprisingly the time went by quickly. I would occasionally look over at the yellow liquid and then think about what it was doing. *This is going to save my life by killing the cancer cells. It might make me sick, but it is obviously worth it.*

The little and the big hand of the clock both pointed to the six. The shift would be in the process of changing soon, and Kara popped in my room and told me she was going home for the night.

My night nurse came in about thirty minutes later. His name was Mark, and he was a little taller than me. At the same time an extremely tall care assistant with dark hair named

Meghan came in and took my vitals before Mark examined me. They were both young adults and they were both very kind.

By the time Mark had finished explaining that I needed to pee every two hours, I was sound asleep. To my memory, this would be the earliest time I ever got to sleep at Children's Mercy because I naturally woke up several times during the night to pee.

Monday morning came around, and a doctor with a moustache and glasses entered my room, residents and nurse practitioners in secession behind him.

"Hi Jonathan, I am Dr. Wicklund," he said. "I wanted to see how you are feeling this morning."

A tan-skinned nurse practitioner named Shirley, who had a voluminous voice, asked me, "As long as you are peeing, pooping, eating and drinking alright then we can discharge you!"

My heart swelled with joy and I told them that I felt pretty well.

"Do you think that I could go to a New Year's Eve lock-in tonight?" I asked with excitement.

"As long as you are feeling OK, you should be fine if you get good sleep and you don't do too much at once," the doctor said. "Your blood counts will start dropping tomorrow at some point, though. Make sure you rest if you are getting worn out."

The following events helped me learn what it would truly mean to understand your limits. The only one who knew what was about to happen was God, and that night, I was reinforced with the idea that I was not some superhero. I was just a kid used to being healthy who *thought* he was invincible.

Chapter 5: Epiphany

Dedicated to: The apostle Paul

The Holy Bible contains many stories, but none of them are quite as fascinating as the story of Saul. He persecuted Christians, and then one day, God made him go blind. Saul promised God that he would change his ways, and God gave him back his sight. Saul's name was changed to Paul, and he had a mission. He became one of God's most reliable servants, and that is what I strive to be. Before I was diagnosed with cancer, I considered myself a Christian. Like a lot of teens, I would fight with my parents and do things that were dishonorable in God's eyes, and yet He still had love for me. In November 2007, I was awakened after being diagnosed, and the most important decision I have ever made was to put my fight with cancer in God's hands. It went from being a burden to becoming one of the greatest blessings I have ever had.

Epiphany

A discovery I have made in my life is that even though you try to do some things a certain way, they don't always end up the way you want them to. This particular New Year's Eve was one that related to this discovery and really showed me something.

My youth group is a huge support system for me. I was so excited to see everyone, and I was going to go to the lock-in no matter what. We met with our sister youth group at their church, and everyone was in sleepover attire. Girls were carrying bags and pillows and so were the guys. There was a great sense of hyper-activity among the whole group, and I could tell it was going to be a long night.

Everyone loaded up into their church vans and we headed toward Bump City, a gymnasium with all kinds of equipment, trampolines, and fun things for teenagers to do. Even though I could only watch people have fun from a distance, I just enjoyed being with all of my friends.

There was a balcony looking down on the rest of the gym, and that's where all the pizza, pop, and junk food were located. I wore my hat to cover my head and my crutches were next to me. It's funny, because when other people do not have to use crutches, they love to play with them. Things change once you actually have to depend on them to get around.

The night was a lot of fun because I got to play dodgeball while sitting, and I still nailed some unlucky kids with a ball. Just because my leg was out of commission, didn't mean my arm was impaired. For several hours people played around the gym while I sat in the balcony and caught up with friends that I hadn't seen in a while. Occasionally I would look around and see kids grinning and jumping. By using crutches, my upper body strength was getting stronger. I used to be able to do things to work out like crunches and one-armed push-ups. When I got cancer, I figured out pretty quickly how little that mattered. Now I would just be grateful to run, let alone walk again. I would have to wait a while for that wish to come true.

Around midnight, sleeping bags were unfurled on the gym floor. Youth leaders' bags in the middle separated the boys and girls. They unrolled a giant screen and started playing a movie.

New Year's Eve is supposed to be about counting down to the start of the New Year, but rarely in my 17 years (16 at the time) on this earth have I seen people paying attention to it. At Bump City it was already 2008 before anyone realized we missed the countdown. Nobody really cared about the official countdown, so we turned off the lights and started watching "Finding Nemo." I had seen it too many times so I just sat down and talked to one of my friends. We probably talked for thirty minutes or so and then a group of friends came over and started talking to me. Surrounded by friends, I remembered the words of John 13:34-35. *"A new command I give you: Love one another. As I have loved you, so you must love one another. By this all men will know that you are my disciples, if you love one another."*

By the time "Finding Nemo" was finished, it was around 2 a.m. and I felt tired. Wendy, the youth pastor from the other church told me that I should go to bed.

"I will be fine," I said with a confident smile.

"Didn't you tell your parents that you should go to sleep?" she said with a skeptical laugh.

I honestly thought that I would go to sleep, but then they put in the next movie: "Coach Carter." It was too late for me to notice that people around me were sneezing and coughing a lot, and it was now 3:45. I needed to go to bed. Then, of all the times to show one of my favorite movies, "Remember the Titans." Then, of all times, they showed one of my favorite movies, "Remember the Titans." I have probably seen it more than any movie. I know many of the lines, so sometimes I narrate the movie when I watch it with my friends. I finally fell asleep around 5:30 and they turned the lights back on at 6. I tried to cover my eyes with my jacket, but someone walked by while they were cleaning up the gym and lifted it off of my head.

When I stood up 15 minutes later I felt like a zombie. I could barely grasp the crutches in my hands because of fatigue. Regret was already starting to remind me that I couldn't afford to lose sleep. My energy is already low enough, why did I only get 30 minutes of sleep? Well, quite frankly, I was an idiot. We drove back to our sister church and 40 or more exhausted, droopy-eyed teens filed inside. The *first* thing I needed to do when I got home was to go to sleep.

My mom picked me up and asked if I had fun. "Y…y…yeah it was a…a…a lot of fun."

I could barely string together a sentence. We arrived home and I feebly crutched into my room as my mom brought me the sports section of the newspaper. I tried to keep my eyes open but I was unsuccessful. I instantly fell asleep and woke up around noon. It was a bitterly cold day and I did not get out of bed because my body said: *Don't get up, you need to rest!*

There were often times during my treatment where I would ignore what my body told me. *I can do this, I am not that tired.*

Two things ultimately led to problems that day. I decided to type "thank you" letters to everyone in the Chambers choir for coming to carol at our house in mid-December, and I did not realize how difficult a task it was event to get up our staircase with crutches. I managed after about five minutes of "one step-at-a-time" maneuvering. I got on the computer and started typing. About four of five letters were written before I started to feel weak. I went to my brother Nathan's room and lay down on his bed.

Nathan is my second oldest brother. He turned twenty on January 28, 2008 and at the time he was a junior at Santa Clara University near San Jose, CA. Nathan is smart, funny, and a lover of music. He plays guitar, drums, and piano. I don't know where I would be without him and my brother Samuel's support.

I decided to finish the typed notes later so I went downstairs and rested on the recliner in the family room and spent the rest of the day watching some TV. The next day I slept in until noon and I was still tired out of my mind. Owen gave me a call and we decided that we wanted to go to Applebee's to watch Georgia play Hawaii in the Fiesta Bowl.

The game was one-sided and I was not feeling much better. My turkey & bacon ciabatta didn't taste that great, and for some reason, I ordered this rich, chocolate brownie and ice cream dessert. My stomach was more than full, yet the cramps went away.

When we got back to my house, Owen helped me get out of the car because it was slippery. The last thing I needed was to slip and break something. Inside it was fairly dark and my parents were in the family room watching a movie. I told them I wasn't feeling too good so my mom helped me get ready for bed. My dog, Dylan, thought that it would be OK if he "helped" by leaping up on the bed and he scratched my blanket. My mom quickly intervened and picked him up. She kissed me goodnight and I fell asleep.

I was woken up by a weird, queasy feeling in my stomach. *Uh-oh.* I looked around and couldn't find anything to throw up in. I vomited for almost three minutes. My body was shaking and I was gasping for breath. I was sweating and my face was pale. My parents came in to my room and sympathized with me.

"Sorry, buddy," said my mom, followed by dad.

My mom got a washcloth and I put it on my forehead. I started feeling sick again. My dad grabbed a bin and handed it to me. While I was heaving, my mom went and got a dissolvable anti-nausea tablet. I wiped off my mouth and put the Zofran underneath my tongue. It made me gag because it tasted like a grape-flavored chewable vitamin, and the next time I threw up it came right back out.

"Maybe we need to go to the hospital," I told them.

At 11:25 I hopped into my dad's car and we were on our way to the E.R. On the way, I held the bin on my lap. Six or seven times I had thrown up before we parked in the handicapped spot right by the Children's Mercy E.R. My dad ran and grabbed a wheelchair and helped me get into the building as I put on a green mask that covered my face and nose. In one hand he held my crutches, and my suitcase was in the other.

Right as we entered, I took off my mask and barfed again. He went straight up to the desk and told them what was wrong. Luckily we were admitted into an examination room right when we got there because they saw me throw up. Vitals were checked and I was running a very high temperature. After five minutes they collected blood samples and they also took cultures to see if I was infected. *Dear God, please help me not to be infected.* They sent in a doctor once they started giving me fluids. She had a very determined, yet soft voice that was soothing to the ears. "The E.R. is no fun, but hopefully we will have a room cleaned up on your floor shortly," she said.

We thanked the doctor and waited about twenty minutes for the nurse to bring some IV medicine to help ease the nausea. Shortly after she gave it to me I fell back asleep. Eventually I felt the table being moved but I just kept my eyes closed. They rolled me from the E.R. to the elevator, and then once again I fell asleep.

A nurse examining me with a stethoscope waked me up. Mom was beside my bed and I realized I was up on 4 Henson. Dad had gone home for the night and my mom helped me take my shoes off. They had been on my feet for several hours in the E.R. while I was lying down. I slowly drifted off to sleep.

I woke up to the noise of the nurse practitioner Shirley's voice. "You missed us so much that you wanted to come back and see us again?!" she yelled, laughing.

The clock read 9:23 a.m. and Shirley talked to my mom about my meds. I could tell she was a very humorous but considerate woman, and all of a sudden it hit me.

In the midst of the dark times of your life, reach out to Jesus. If you let Him enter your heart then he will watch over you and take care of you. This place (Children's Mercy) will be like a second home and the people here will be like a second family over the next nine months. Embrace them and love them because they love you. The Lord my God is with me always if I commit my life to Him.'

That was when I realized I needed to re-dedicate my life. I needed to live for Christ and tell other people about Him. I can use this story to spread His Word, and that is what I am trying to do.

I talked to my mom about how I was feeling and I tried eating some crackers. They stayed down so I started eating some more. There was a knock on the door and one of the nutritionists came in to talk about my eating.

"When you first came in, your weight was in the 150-155 lb. range," she explained. "It has dropped significantly to 139, and if it gets down past 135 you will have lost 10% of your body weight. I am not trying to scare you, but if we can't get your weight back up we will have to insert a (nasogastric) tube through your nose and feed you with a drip that runs into your stomach. The NG tube allows you to get liquid food into your system." *I need to get my weight back up because I do not want an NG tube installed. That sounds like no fun at all.*

The dietician explained some different ways I could get my weight up. One of her ideas involved "Scandi shakes," which were basically packed with calories. She talked to my mom in the hall and I felt something in my mouth similar to a canker sore. The bottom of my tongue and the sides of my mouth all had little cuts. One of the main side effects of Methotrexate was oral mucositis (mouth sores). This was the beginning of the most painful experience I had ever had.

Dr. Shore came into the room and asked me what I thought about the KU football team's chances in the Orange Bowl.

"KU will win, but I think it will be close," I said.

"I think Virginia Tech is pretty good so we'll see about that," he said laughing.

The game started at 7:00 but I kept dozing off to sleep. My night nurse gave me IV Benadryl, which knocked me out. I woke up during the end of the fourth quarter and saw KU winning, 24-21, and I fell asleep in a good mood.

A nurse with short brown hair and blue eyes was checking my breathing the next morning and she introduced herself. Her name was Leslie and she was one nurse who was always so efficient. If I had any nausea, she would order the medication lickity-split. As a patient you appreciate that because **you know that they really care about your health and how you feel.**

On this day I also met Jennie. She was a C.A. who had glasses, short blond hair, and the ability to make laugh until my sides hurt. Jennie had a fiancé named Joe, a great guy, and he was a C.A. on the floor as well. Together they would always be such great friends to me when I was at CMH.

Over the next few days I was still being taken care of by Leslie and Jennie and one day I got very sick. Leslie came in and asked Jennie if I had a fever. I didn't but I was definitely burning up.

My mom was out doing errands, and I was alone when there was a knock on the door. Someone from the Child Psychology Department entered and asked if I would be interested in trying out therapy. They told me I would try it out upon discharge from the floor. *Therapy? I hope it helps me to get my nausea under control.* I couldn't eat without my mouth hurting now because there were noticeable white sores on the inside of my mouth. My nausea was getting better, however.

Leslie came into my room and noticed that I was having trouble drinking a Scandi shake through a straw. I tried to conceal the grimaces on my face but I failed.

"If you want something for your mouth pain I would be happy to get it for you, Jonathan!" she offered.

I nodded my head yes because it was painful to talk. She came back in and saw my Bible next to my bed.

"Are you a believer?" she asked me.

"I am," I told her. "I know God is watching over me."

We started talking about faith in God and she asked me about myself. I told her about my choir and some other things, and she was so kind. Our conversation lasted about 45 minutes and I asked toward the end if there were other patients she needed to take care of. She told me that she wanted to make sure I was OK first because I had nausea and I was by myself for a little while. "God has you here for a reason, and I believe whole-heartedly that it is His plan for me to help take care of you," she told me.

I was finally discharged but felt a little nauseated. We went down to see if therapy would help. To make a long story short, I figured out what caused me to throw up in certain situations. When I felt nauseated, my body would have a reaction that caused stress. They told me that when the psychological result of feeling queasy came on my body temperature would rise. How could I control it?

Breathing. This became very important later on. What happened next was one of the most painful things I have gone through, but after I was through with it, I had never felt more healed in my life.

Chapter 6: Faith

Dedicated to: Job

Is there a time where you feel like things are pretty rocky? If so, you should read the book of Job. The devil thought Job would turn his back on God if his most prized possessions were taken away from him. So God said, you can take everything away from Job but life itself. The Devil killed Job's family, the animals that provided his meals, and made Job extremely sick. Job was almost to the point of death, and he knew that he was not strong enough to carry on alone. Ultimately, Job could have turned his back on God and cursed his name, and yet, he praised Him. Instead of never talking to God again, Job prayed more. His faith in an almost fatal situation is something that inspired me to trust God no matter what. God loves me, and I know that He will never give me more than I can handle. It is my firm belief that God used cancer as a way to change my life, and even the lives of people around me for the better.

Faith

We left the hospital on a freezing January day and arrived home.

I saw my dog Dylan and couldn't help but grin. I decided to have chemotherapy given the next day because I didn't want to get off schedule. My mouth was sore from Methotrexate and I realized that it would be more painful once round three was under my belt. God gave me strength to dive head first into the unknown. I looked at the bright side: I might have some mouth sores but didn't have any nausea, and that was a blessing. I believed that God would get me through the next few weeks because He got me through the last couple of weeks.

The third round of treatment would start the next day. My parents were worried about starting more chemotherapy when I was just getting over being sick, but I had one thing that gave me the drive to carry on: faith. I was not counting at the time, but I had four rounds left before my total knee replacement surgery. *The faster I can get through it, the better.* Lots of prayers, visits, and anti-nausea drugs would help push me along.

My mouth was a little sorer when I opened my eyes that January morning. I got out of bed and stretched, feeling the cold air envelope me and raise each and every hair on my body. Packing the suitcase was a very difficult process because I could barely move. We went to the garage and it was so cold it felt like we were in an igloo. We hopped in the mini-van and I bundled up in a blanket, trying not to freeze before I arrived at the hospital.

The parking lot is divided into four different levels: Red Rocket (1st floor), Yellow Submarine (2nd floor), Purple Plane (3rd floor), & Turquoise Train (4th floor). Since it was early on a Thursday morning, we parked on Red Rocket and got in the elevator that takes you up to the clinic on floor 2.

At 8:20 we said hello to Anna and Ryan, who were working at the desk. They let Kaylynne know I was there and five minutes later she opened the door and took me to the height/weight room to do vitals. My blood pressure was high even after the second time she checked and my weight was down. Rochelle entered our waiting room a few minutes later.

"How do you feel? Did you enjoy your day off?" she said with a cautious laugh.

"Yeah it was definitely nice to be home, even if it was only for a day," I said.

She removed the numbing cream from my port and cleaned off my access site.

"Do you want me to count?"

I nodded and she counted to three and inserted the needle into my skin. For the first time the stick slightly hurt. I winced but I told her I was fine so she proceeded with the other butterfly needle. Once it was inserted she drew labs.

She made sure the port was working all right first. The port-cleaning solution they use always gave me a funny taste in my mouth (which is weird because it wasn't in my mouth). She drew blood into a waste tube so she would get clean samples. Two other tubes were used to collect blood. She rinsed my port then hooked me up to the IV pole so I could begin pre-hydration.

I put my earphones in and I pressed the "shuffle" button. Slowly my eyelids closed and I was asleep. When I woke up, it was around noon and Kaylynne asked if I wanted a snack or something to drink.

Cheetos became a common junk food that I indulged in both in the clinic and up on 4-H. The only problem with Cheetos is that they leave your fingertips orange and cheesy. The fluids had been running for about three hours and I was so dehydrated from not drinking regularly (it hurt to drink with mouth sores) that I hadn't had to go to the bathroom yet. Rochelle came in and replaced the bag of fluids with another bag.

I started receiving chemo at about 3:30, so I was scheduled to finish around 7:30. My dad encouraged me to order something to eat, so I ordered a burrito from the cafeteria. The burrito was OK but it made my stomach feel weird. I turned on the TV and my care assistant Jessica poked her head in and asked me: "Can you pee for me? I need a sample every two hours so you might not get a ton of sleep tonight."

This was what they always had to do when I received Methotrexate. She thanked me after I gave her a sample in one of the plastic urinals. Every time you pee they dip into it with a syringe and check the chemistries and find out if you are dehydrated and what your pH level is.

At six o'clock my parents went to the Parents' Room down the hall on the other side of the floor to get a quick bite to eat. Before they left, I was watching TV when I heard a knock on my door. The door opened and a woman with pulled-back red hair and big eyes poked her head around the curtain.

"Are you Jonathan?" asked a very gentle voice.

"Yeah that's me," I said smiling.

"I am Brooke, one of the volunteers! I am here every Thursday night. I just wanted to see if there's anything I can bring you? There are pop, chips, cookies, ravioli, Lunchables, etc. Is there anything you want?"

"If you get the chance I would love to have a Lunchable," I said with a guilty smile.

"I will be back with that in a minute," she said, smiling at my parents.

Brooke is an example of someone who helped me get through my hospital stays every time I went in. I always got admitted on Thursdays so I would get to see her (later in my treatment when I wasn't so sick it was something I looked forward to even more). Before she left around 10 she came in and asked if there was anything else I needed. I told her I was fine and she said she would see me next time.

The next morning Matt, one of the staff psychologists, paid me a visit. Matt had short, dark hair and he was probably in his late twenties or early thirties. We started talking and we discussed how he typically helped kids deal with extreme nausea.

"There is a breathing method I can teach you that will eventually help you control your nausea if you work on it," he told me.

Anything that will help lessen the nausea I am willing to try. We talked for about 30 minutes and he gave me his business card so I would have his number in case I needed anything.

Several days passed and the nausea persisted, so I wasn't eating much at all. On that next Tuesday my Methotrexate level was low enough that I could leave, but I was not able to quite yet. My mouth was in pain even though the Phenergan helped keep the nausea under control. To help get through this they gave me pain pills called Oxycontin and Oxycodone, as well as an orange mouthwash that I could swallow called Nystatin.

Nystatin supposedly helped numb the pain in your mouth as well as fight off infection. They said I could go home as long as I kept drinking fluids and eating as much as I could.

We got home on January 16 and I was exhausted. My tutor was scheduled to come and do a session for math. I was eager to begin homebound schooling because I wanted to keep up with the rest of my classmates and graduate on time. In the afternoon a very friendly, middle-aged teacher with brown hair and glasses came to my house.

Throughout my whole session with her I struggled to sit up straight. She was very nice though and she understood I was tired. We scheduled to meet again the next day.

"Isn't it great that we are home?" my mom asked me.

I couldn't talk very well but I told her that I *was* very happy to be home. The day dragged on and on and I took a pain pill for my mouth.

That night my grandmother, Boz (her real name is Barbara), and my brother Sam came over to eat dinner with us. I sat and watched, and I hadn't eaten anything but crackers, applesauce, and shakes for the last week or so. Midway through dinner my stomach started acting up, so I went to my room and lay down. I did not feel well at all. An hour or so passed and I tried getting to sleep. I was unsuccessful but my brother left a note with a butterfly on it.

Hey Juice,

I am sorry you aren't feeling too well. I know you are sick but it was still great to see you tonight. I just want to tell you how proud of you I am. You are looking good, buddy. We have no idea what you are going through, but we want you to know that we are there for you every step of the way. I love you so much and I pray for you every day.

Love,
Samuel

P.S. I hope this butterfly will help make you feel better.

This note from my brother meant so much to me that I read it several times before falling asleep.

I woke up feeling incredible pain. I took some Nystatin and another pill and it gave me a little bit of relief. My parents said I should let them know if I thought we needed to go to the hospital. I did not sleep very well and the next day I could barely get out of bed. I decided to try and take my mind off the pain by finishing the thank you notes to the Chambers singers. This took a lot more energy than I originally anticipated. Before my tutor came over I tried drinking a fruit smoothie. My mouth hurt so much that the pulp that hadn't been grinded up from the shake got caught in my teeth and I started to cry. If I moved my tongue to where the pulp was stuck I felt even more pain. I went and looked in a mirror at the inside of my mouth. Every corner of it was spotted with white sores under my tongue, on the sides of my mouth, and on my gums. Dad called the hospital and we rushed over. We went to the clinic and they gave me a bolus (fast-acting pain relief) of pain medicine after they accessed the port, and I had never appreciated a pain reliever more. The relief didn't last long.

"You have really bad mucositis and you have really low counts," Dr. Shore told me. "I am not going to tell you that you have to be admitted, but if you are in a lot of pain, then it probably would not be a bad idea."

I pondered what to do for about five seconds and thought: *I know I won't get as much time away from the hospital before my next admission but the right thing to do is to stay here and get the pain under control.*

"I think I need to be admitted," I said, somehow managing to get a whole sentence out.

Dr. Shore thought that I had made a wise decision. It took a while to get up to the floor but we made it up eventually. Strangely I ended up in Room 19 again. Mandy came into my room and saw that I was in a lot of pain.

I was put on a fentanyl drip, and for that next week, I was out of it. Round 4 was supposed to start on January 24 so I decided to go ahead and just do it. They were already pre-hydrating me and once the chemistries were right, my nurse hung the bag of Cisplatin.

The day that they started the chemo, they told me that they needed to use an IV in my arm. One of my ports was used for the pain drip. The other was used for pre-hydration and anti-nausea medication. In my room was my mom, the float nurse, another nurse, Jennie my C.A. and her fiancé, Joe. The nurse told me she would count to three and then put in the IV with the needle. She tried on the top of my left wrist but it wouldn't go in. My eyes started watering and Jennie had her hands on my shoulders while Joe tried to talk to me and distract me from the pain. Mom was on the right of me hugging me. The float nurse said she was looking for a big vein and she pulled the IV out. She tried me again and missed, causing my eyes to run with tears. I could handle the pain but in my head I said: *God, please help her find the right vein to the put the IV in.* She apologized nervously and pulled the IV out again.

She would try one more time and was unsuccessful. At this point I started to cry a little bit and the float nurse said she couldn't deal with causing any more pain. She left with the other nurse and I wept a little harder. They said they would bring an IV team up to put in the IV. Jennie hugged me for a few minutes and Joe could barely watch. After Jennie and Joe left the room I bawled. My mom held me in her arms and I didn't stop crying until the IV team came in fifteen minutes later. It took them about a minute to find a big enough vein and then they inserted the IV smoothly. I thanked them and my nurse came in and unclamped the chemo line so it would start running.

The next few days were not easy. The nutritionist and Dr. Shore wanted me to try a pill called Marinol, which is used as an appetite-stimulant and an anti-nausea medicine. Marinol is a derivative of marijuana, and it gave me the same buzz someone feels when they get high. It constantly gave me the desire to eat, but it helped with nausea so I kept using it.

One day Mandy was taking care of me and it was getting close to the end of the day shift. I was asleep and dad was in my room. When I woke up I turned on the TV. There was a college basketball game on and I was excited to watch. At first I had a happy expression on my face and then it turned into one that was warped with confusion. About a minute passed and I turned off the TV. "Where am I?" I asked my dad.

"You are in the hospital getting chemotherapy and pain relief," he said.

"How long have I been here?" I asked.

"You have been here for a while."

I started to cry and I repeated those two questions over and over. I looked around the room and since I had been in it for practically a couple of weeks straight, it felt like I had been in there for an eternity.

"Do you want me to get Mandy?"

"No, but where am I?" asked at an elevated volume. "This doesn't make any sense!"

He went out and got Mandy to come in my room because he knew her presence would help my emotions get in check.

"Are you OK, Jonathan?" she asked. "You have been in this room for a while."

When she began to talk to me I snapped out of the weird trance I had been in. The fentanyl drip and the Marinol had caused me to tweak out.

Mandy was someone who I could joke around with, but she was not someone who I was prepared to cry in front of. Her personality was one that is very calming when you are in pain, and very amusing when you are sitting back and trying to find something to keep you from being bored.

I was neutropenic for the next several days so they had to give me blood. I had a fever while I was getting the blood infusion, so my nurse Manda had to wear a mask, gloves, and a yellow gown into my room. My youth pastor, Kyle, visited me during the infusion because it took four hours. He found out I couldn't talk or move my mouth due to mouth sores and so I had a pain drip. He learned the pain drip and the Cisplatin caused extreme nausea, and for that I took Marinol and Benadryl. The Marinol gave me a desire to eat but when I did I would throw up. It was a vicious cycle and my weight was dropping like a lead balloon.

"I can't imagine how tough this is, but I promise you can get through it. You don't want that thing stuck down your nose," Kyle told me. "It is bad now, but it would be worse having to deal with that. You need to eat no matter what."

He was very sincere and before he left we both were crying together. He prayed with me and gave me reassurance that I could persevere. They were already giving me nutrition through my port, which was a way to keep my weight up, but it had the risk of having an infection. Kyle's words: "Eat no matter what," stuck with me.

That night, Ricky the pharmacist came in with a shot called a G-CSF (Granulocyte colony-stimulating factor) – the shot I would take once each day for about four days. It didn't hurt when they stuck it in the right thigh. Ricky even taught me how to give myself the shot. It slowly caused the white blood count to increase so that my body could fight off the bacteria in my mouth (eventually getting rid of the mouth sores). The goal was for my immune system to be able to fight off possible infections. There was one huge side effect that I didn't know about initially. Late that night my bones started aching. Each day a different bone would hurt if I even touched that part of my body. The first night it was my tailbone. I was so skinny from weight loss that it stuck out. I could not sleep on my back or sit in one position for more than five minutes at a time because the pain was excruciating. The next day my left shoulder hurt, followed by my feet. I started weaning off the fentanyl drip but was constipated. One night I went to the bathroom and could not go, no matter how hard I tried. In frustration I crutched back to my bed and slammed one of the bedposts while letting out some choice words. I ended up making the pain worse by hitting my hand on the side of the bed. My dad told me never to do that again, and I never did.

My right shoulder hurt already as I tried a red spray that was supposed to soothe the pain from my mouth sores. I squirted it in my mouth and instead of relief, I experienced what felt like a burning sensation. I screamed in literal agony for what seemed like much more than a matter of moments, and my dad ran over and told me to be quiet. He did not realize how much pain I was in. I feebly reached out my arms and then he knew exactly what was wrong. As he rushed to embrace me, we both started crying. At that moment I remembered Psalm 121:1-8.

"I lift up my eyes to the hills — where does my help come from? My help comes from the Lord, the Maker of heaven and earth. He will not let your foot slip — he who watches over you will not slumber; indeed, he who watches over Israel will neither slumber nor sleep. The Lord watches over you — the Lord is your shade at your right hand; the sun will not harm you by day, nor the moon by night. The Lord will keep you from all harm — he will watch over your life; the Lord will watch over your coming and going both now and forevermore."

Tonight might not be my night, but I know that things are going to get better.

Days passed away like seconds as I look back, but each one individually seemed like a week at a time.

Eventually I found the light at the end of tunnel, as I was convinced to get back to eating. Even though it was difficult with the pains in my mouth, my nurses helped me. Mandy was there encouraging me to drink and eat, and eventually the counts came back up and the pain was under control with the help of medication.

The white sores that were inside my cheeks and under my tongue came out one night while I was eating ravioli, and I do not know if I have ever felt so relieved. I could again move my tongue around the inside of my mouth without feeling pain. My mouth was once again smooth instead of ripped up, so I could eat normally and gain weight back bit by bit. The day I left the floor some people came up and gave me hugs, and others just looked at me and smiled. As Kay Yow, the North Carolina State women's basketball coach who beat cancer, once said: "When life kicks you, let it kick you forward."

At that point I thought: *I had zero control over getting cancer, but I have 100 percent control over how I respond to having cancer.* January prepared me to attempt to deal with everything in life by trying to use kindness and patience.

As I was wheeled toward the exit of the floor and toward the elevators, I looked back and thanked God. Before I exited I thanked Mandy, because at that moment I knew that she was one of the reasons that I was now leaving the floor. She was one of the many nurses who would help me see this thing through.

Chapter 7: Goals

Dedicated to: Cross Country Coach Tricia Beaham

The time: freshman year of high school; the place: Village Presbyterian Church; the fool: me. Here I am, it is not even the first day of cross country practice, and I thought I could keep up with senior John McCormick and the varsity squad. I am stopped at the church down the street from school, gasping for air and dying of thirst. My idea of keeping up with a thoroughbred group of runners was not a goal, it was a death wish. As I waited to drink from the water fountain, one of my brother's friends, Graham Stark, told me to keep up with him for the remainder of the 5-mile route. I kept up with him and ended up earning a spot on the JV squad several weekends later. My coach, Tricia, told me how far I had come in so short an amount of time, and encouraged me to keep setting goals to strive for. My senior year I became one of the captains of my cross country team. Tricia helped me learn the importance of hard work, and told me if I always worked hard I could not be disappointed because I had given things my best shot. I took this to heart and worked hard to get through homebound tutoring while I was doing treatment. Tricia burned me an inspirational CD and wrote me a card of encouragement. I owe her a lot, and feel so blessed that she had such a positive impact on my life!

Goals

Don't Let it Pass You By

Time is a scary word to some.
It passes slowly, yet it goes by in the blink of an eye.
It will stop eventually, right?
All we can do is make the most out of the time given to us.
If we do that, does it matter if time stops?
Time will always exist, it's our own time on Earth that ends at some point.
We cannot waste a minute, because life is short.

Hospitalization for several weeks at a time is both physically and mentally draining. Once my tutors started coming almost every week things got a little tougher. I had a one-hour session with Ms. Hart on Tuesdays for math, and I had two-hour sessions with Ms. Burkhardt on Wednesdays for English and American History. The first semester I had received an A in Math so I made a goal to get an A again. It was the same goal for English and history: try to get an A and don't make excuses.

I met Ms. Burkhardt one day and she brought The Adventures of Huckleberry Finn. I would have loved reading the whole thing with my own two eyes but unfortunately I couldn't stay focused and alert for that long.

"I know you are probably pretty tired from treatment, so I am going to give you the cassette tape that is narrated by

Garrison Keillor," she said. "That way you can listen and not worry about getting all of the reading completed."

That was an act of kindness she performed without ever knowing me. I was happy that both of my tutors were such nice people. They were working to help achieve my goals. After she gave me the book, she started reading with me and slowly I started getting drowsy. Ms. Burkhardt's voice was very melodic and I figured out very quickly that I would have to battle to stay awake (and not because it was boring). A large portion of our first session involved discussing English and then we moved on to history at the end of our time. I said goodbye to my tutor after she had filled out the next assignment sheet.

My first instinct was to go to our recliner in the family room and take a nap, but my conscience told me I could finish my English assignment right then and there. *If you get it finished now you won't have to stress about it later.* I tried reading and listening to the first third of the book that afternoon. I try to be organized, and even with being slowed down by the cancer, I didn't want that to change. Work fast, play later is the way that I lived my life. I almost made it through the first third of the book but then I fell asleep reading. I later awoke to our dog jumping on my leg.

"Dylan! Get off!" I yelled. "Mom, please call Dylan!"

Once I yelled he immediately jumped down. This was one time where I wasn't too happy with him.

The next couple of days I prayed that I wouldn't have to go to the hospital before the fifth round of chemo. As each day passed, I knew that God had heard my prayers. I actually felt pretty good. *My stamina is a little bit better than when I was in the hospital.* I was beginning my third month on crutches and my arms were getting used to my legs not doing all the work. People asked me if my armpits hurt, but surprisingly they didn't. It is amazing how weak certain areas of my body became and how strong other parts of my body grew. I was exercising a lot of muscles in my upper back that aren't normally doing much.

I could make this comparison to my faith, because I never before realized how much God had blessed me throughout my life. I would often take things for granted, whether it is my health, getting an education, or having friends by my side. At the time I didn't have as much physical strength, but it was my goal to get it back one day. I had to work harder to get an education because I wouldn't be in school. I would try to get through the semester with the help of the tutors. I wanted to keep up with my class so that I could graduate in the spring of 2009. The Lord blessed me with such helpful tutors and I felt equipped to do just that. *Cancer is not going to hold me back. I will just work harder when I have more energy.* I then thought of all the kids that could not even go to school. What would it be like not to meet kids and make friends? I had been going to school for ten and a half years with a large group of kids, and to not see them every day would be so hard.

Days passed, and for once, time seemed to speed up. Every day my parents reminded me that there were only two rounds of chemo left before a six-week break. This was like a beam of sunshine bursting through a cloudy sky. *Only two rounds of chemo left before my exodus from the hospital.*

A large decision had come up in my treatment when I arrived at the hospital for my third infusion of Methotrexate.

"Last time you received Methotrexate you became nauseated on top of having mouth sores," Dr. Shore explained. "We are trying to find a regimen of anti-nausea meds that work for you.

The Kytril and Benadryl seem to help on a temporary basis, but you don't like the Marinol or the Ativan."

"We can keep looking for different meds, but one option is being put on a Diprivan pump," Dr. Shore said. "We basically put you to sleep when you get admitted for chemo. That way you wouldn't have to be miserable throwing up, but that is a last resort. We will use Kytril, Phenergan, and Benadryl for this round and then maybe we can make a decision."

Wretched Winter

Sitting here frozen
One of the chosen
Each day is fleeting
I am passed by.

Lit up by the daytime
Enshrouded by night
My body is still
Yet my mind is in flight.

This is not the beginning
But the end's not near
One thing, however,
Is glaringly clear.

I am combating the cold
Running the race
The war makes me old
The finish I'll embrace.

I cannot go outside,
The ground's coated with snow
Four rounds are complete
Only fourteen to go.

Like clockwork, Brooke walked into my room. At the same time, my night nurse, Kelly, came in and asked me a question.

"There is a boy named Nick who would really like to meet you, but he can't leave his room," she said. "If you want to meet him just let me know."

"He is pretty sick," said Brooke.

Unfortunately I wouldn't be able to meet him until he was feeling better. Kelly brought in my chemo and she gave me Kytril before she hung it up on the IV pole.

Brooke sat down in a recliner next to me. My parents were out having dinner after I convinced them I would be fine by myself for a while. The Benadryl always affected me within minutes of being injected into the IV line. Kelly told me she would be back when my IV pole started beeping.

"Do you feel anything when it goes in?" Brooke asked.

"No, I can't feel a thing," I told her. "It is usually several days later that I start getting side effects."

Brooke asked me another question and I started to answer but I babbled off about something totally unrelated to what she asked. Being as nice as she was, she just nodded her head as I said whatever sputtered out. This would not be the last time I fell asleep while Brooke was visiting the floor.

I woke up, turned to my right, and Brooke was still there. She must have been bored while I was asleep, but it was so nice of her to stay.

"Hey, you can go back to sleep if you're tired," she said. "I will see you next week, bud."

Brooke waved goodbye and I instantly fell asleep.

When I woke throughout the night to pee I was excited. Why was I excited? I was feeling well. I was really fatigued, but I was happy I was keeping the food down.

The next night I set a record for how late I stayed up. I watched TV until about 2:30 in the morning. One of the nurses, Amy, was taking care of me that night, and she came in to see how I was doing.

"Why are you still up?" she said with a laugh.

"I have energy for some reason, and I am really hungry."

"Do you want a snack?" she offered.

I ended up eating a lot of junk food because my stomach felt like a bottomless pit.

At around 3:00, I fell asleep. The rest of the weekend went very well because I only had a little bit of an upset stomach. I had established that I enjoyed staying up late. From then on the night shift considered me a night owl.

Sleep is important, and I would often doze off when tired, but in ten months at Children's Mercy I only took two planned naps. That is how much I loved talking to everyone, and it was my goal to establish lasting friendships with the people who God placed in my life to care for me.

Philippians 4:13 says: *"I can do everything through Him who gives me strength."* I could accomplish this feat by getting through my surgery and the next 13 rounds of chemo. *I cannot quit, and I will not quit. I will not only survive, but will also thrive with God helping me.*

Chapter 8: Hope

Dedicated to: University of Kansas Men's Head Basketball Coach Bill Self

Everybody knows that Coach Self is widely regarded as one of the best coaches in the game of college basketball today. He has won a National Championship and set the school record for wins in only his fifth season leading the Jayhawks. When I met Coach Self in November 2007 before the biggest non-conference home game of the year (Arizona), I was in awe. My mom and dad pushed me into the entrance of Allen Fieldhouse in a wheelchair and dad told us to wait outside the gym. Mr. Chalmers, the Director of Basketball Operations at the time, came out and introduced himself. He then invited me inside the hallowed room and it was a dream come true. Coach Self was the first person I got to meet.

"Are you ready for this?" he asked in reference to my struggle with cancer.

"Yes sir," I replied.

He got me a seat for the game and told me to make myself comfortable. Then he let me watch the scout team help prepare the rest of the squad for the night's upcoming game. After the team finished practicing, Coach Self told the team and the coaching staff to gather around me. He told them who I was and what was going on, and I said Hi to the team. After he dismissed everyone, every player, and every member of the coaching and training staffs introduced themselves with big smiles on their faces. After the game, Coach Self found me and apologized that the team played such a bad game (even though they won). He gave me his email address and told me to stay in touch. I will never forget that day. Thank you, Coach Self.

Hope

In high school I had been involved in the musical. Freshman year I was in "Grease" and sophomore year I was in "Sweet Charity." In October I had been working with Judy Bliss, the nicest voice teacher, on an audition song to use to try out for "Guys and Dolls." We worked for several weeks in preparation but just when I thought everything was all ready, I got diagnosed.

At first I thought I could still be in it. *I can't dance right now, but I can sing as long as I have enough energy.* I knew I could still go see it in February but this year I would not be on stage for opening night. This was not an easy thing to think about because I would miss all of the fun times the cast shared.

One day in February I got a phone call from Erin, a senior girl who was in choir with me, and who was the lead in the musical.

"Hey Jonathan! How are you?!"

"Hey Erin! I am doing all right, thanks. How are you?"

"I am doing awesome, bud! I was wondering if Katie, Courtney, and I could come over after musical practice tonight. It might be kind of late, though. Our rehearsals have been a little longer because next week is show week."

"I would love that!" I said. "It doesn't matter what time, I will be up," I said.

Around 8:45, I heard the doorbell ring. I got up from one of the chairs in our living room and crutched over to the front door. When I opened it I saw three smiling faces and one by one each girl gave me a big hug.

Courtney's dad, Mr. Pennington, had been a huge inspiration and a great mentor and supporter over the last few months. He had visited with me, prayed with me, and encouraged me to put all my trust in God.

The trio of girls had all been at my house when the Chambers singers came and caroled in the family room in December. Erin and Courtney were both seniors, and Katie a junior. We all talked for several minutes and then something happened that I would never forget.

Courtney pulled a light blue book out of the bag sitting on the floor next to her. She handed it to me and told me it was a gift from Club 121 and choir.

The first message was a note from the choir explaining the gift:

Jonathan,

You are so brave! All of us are proud to know you. Jonathan, look at the influence you have had on these people. With every word you say, action that you take, and round of chemo you beat, you point to Christ and the strength and grace He daily gives you. People recognize you are different, as you will see from these letters, many are realizing that the difference within you is JESUS! That is amazing! We love you! You are in our thoughts and prayers always.

Honored to know you,
Courtney, SME Choir, and SME Club 121

Wow, I thought to myself. *This is one of the nicest gifts anyone has ever given me.* I gave Courtney a big hug and told all three of them that I would see them next Wednesday for the Potluck dinner and performance. After they had all given me a hug they told me they would see me soon.

I stayed in my living room as I watched them walk out to their cars. I started flipping through the book and counted 61 notes. Some that really stood out were from classmates of all different ages.

Courtney's note was the first one I read:

We wanted to give you strength and encouragement that you could read anytime and rest in, knowing that people were supporting you and heaven is flooded with prayers on your behalf. So here is the book, read it day or night and know you are loved. As I spent time compiling these thoughts and prayers for you, the main theme I found was first of all that your faith has been noticed. People are astounded to see the way you have handled yourself and you have truly shown them the Lord through your actions. You have received your strength from above and you are not shy about telling people that. How brave!! All of us are so proud to call you our friends! Another similar theme I found is how everyone finds you so kind and approachable. You are so friendly to every person and are a warm smile in the midst of this hectic and busy life in high school. Everyone is here to support you and cheer for you. Look how many people offered you their numbers and said call anytime night or day! It is beautiful to see our peers come together in support and prayer. Jonathan, you are fighting the fight. I am praying that the Lord continues to give you grace and power for every moment. Lean on Him. Trust in His Word and His promises. He will use this experience in amazing ways. I pray His peace would rest upon you and you would be wrapped in the blanket of His Love.

The Lord your God is with you,
He is mighty to save.
He will take great delight in you,
He will quiet you with His love,
He will rejoice over you with singing.
- Zephaniah 3:17

Love and Prayers, Courtney

The letter after Courtney's that caught my eye was from a senior named Matt.

Jonathan,
You will never know how much everyone cares about you. I cannot help but think about your struggle daily. Each day Harms has to count you absent I cannot help but think and worry about what you are going through. I went to church a few weeks ago, dozing off as normal, and then I heard your name. At first I didn't know what was going on and then I realized you were on the sick list. This is the first time that anyone that I know has been on the sick list, and it hit home, hard. For the rest of mass my thoughts never wandered, I was only thinking about you. I hope I never have to fight what you are beating right now. I don't know if I would be strong enough. But you are strong enough. Stronger than me. Once you are back in class

sitting by me, I would like just one thing from you. A handshake, from the strongest person I know.

Matt

I read several encouraging Bible verses:

Come to me, all you who are weary and burdened, and I will give you rest. Take my yoke upon you and learn from me, for I am gentle and humble in heart, and you will find rest for your souls. For my yoke is easy and my burden is light. –Matthew 11:28-30

When you pass through the waters, I will be with you; and when you pass through the rivers, they will not sweep over you. When you walk through the fire, you will not be burned; the flames will not set you ablaze. –Isaiah 43:2

"With man this is impossible, but with God all things are possible." –Matthew 19:26

The next letter made me cry. But my tears were joyful, not filled with sorrow.

Hey man,

I really hope you're doing all right. I want you to know that I have so much respect for you. I'm realizing more and more what life is. It's very delicate. I see myself and other kids throwing their lives around with drugs and just being stupid. It makes me wonder what it is like to actually fully appreciate life. I can't at all pretend to relate to what you're dealing with, but you and I have been pretty decent mates in the past. If you're EVER bored, text me or call me, dude. I have unlimited texts and I attend Shawnee Mission East, so I'm not going to miss anything if I get the occasional text. Your fight has taught me a lot, and I really think of you whenever I'm about to do something stupid. I don't know what kind of consolation that has, but you're an inspiration, and your courage is so great. I wish I could be that strong.

I look up to you and respect you to no end. You've always been awesome in my eyes and I want you to know we all miss and love you, man.

Keep it up,
Kaevan

I got to the end of the book, and the last two pages had a sweet note from Courtney's cousin: Meg Howland.

Dear Jonathan,
Hey, how are you? I hope you are feeling better. Everyone at school misses you so much! It is weird without you in choir. I know, I know, it sounds weird to say since there are like 129 other kids in that class, but seriously it is strange without you. I'm used to seeing you every day since you're right in my field of vision when I look at the clock. And, let's be honest, I look at the clock a lot in that class. So, now I have no friendly face to look for. I can't wait till you are back again. We're still plugging away at that crazy Handel song, and I'm sure the basses could use your help. But, overall, you haven't missed much. Not like last year with New York. I still remember our

first night there when we went to ESPN Zone. I sat by you, and probably annoyed you, but I had a lot of fun talking to you. That was such a great trip. I'm super jealous that you guys get to take another one next year. That will be so much fun! Anyway, I just wanted to let you know how much I am thinking/praying about you. I know that it is so hard to imagine but God has a plan and he is using this illness. I know that good things will come out of this and God is looking out for you right now. I pray that he'll reveal his plan to you soon, and that plan will be a motivation to you. I know that some good things have come out of this already. For example, you are inspiring all of your classmates every day. When we are faced with a problem all we have to do is remember the strength and perseverance you are using every day. I am stunned by the courage you are using Jonathan, and I pray that you keep it up.

Remember our God can move the mountains, and he will move this mountain from you!! Everyone at school is thinking about you and praying for you. Seriously, people who probably aren't believers are praying right now because they know how much it means to you. That is so amazing to think about! I can't imagine how hard these past few weeks have been, but I hope you know how many people are supporting you. We all love and care about you very much, and we are here whenever you need us. God is in control and "we know that in all good things God works for the good of those who love him, who have been called according to his purpose." Romans 8:28 I think God's words say it best, he is working for your good because you love him, and he will not let you down! I pray that you remember every day how much God loves you and that he is with you even in the hardest times. Take care, and thanks for reading this long rambling letter! I can't wait till you are back in 5th hour with us.

In Him, Meg Howland

At that moment, I felt an overwhelming source of love being sent my way. My peers were so thoughtful and I don't know if any letter that I have ever received meant as much as that little blue book did. . . It was truly an answered prayer. If I needed support or some guidance, I had a reference in addition to the Bible. I felt renewed, but most of all it was hope that I felt, gleaming like a ray of sunshine through a cloud.

Each morning when I wake I say,
"I place my hand in God's today;"
I know He'll walk close by my side
My every wandering step to guide.

He leads me with tender care
When paths are dark and I despair
No need for me to understand
If I but hold fast to His hand.

My hand in His! No surer way
To walk in safety through each day.
By His great bounty I am fed;
Warmed by His love, and comforted.

When at day's end I seek my rest
And realize how much I'm blessed,
My thanks pour out to Him; and then
I place my hand in God's again.

Chapter 9: Inspiration

Dedicated to: Author J.K. Rowling

Before she was known as "richest woman in the world" and "the creator of Harry Potter," she was living in poverty. J.K. Rowling could not afford paper so she would go to coffee shops with her baby and write on napkins. One of the reasons that I decided to write a book is because of her story. She gave me endless hours of joy with her wonderful writing. The magic in her books might not be real, but there is magic to be spared in her ultra-creative cranium. She proved to me that anyone can write if they pour their heart, soul, and mind into it. Rowling is one of my heroes because even though she was at a rock-bottom point in her life, she climbed to something far greater than she ever could have imagined. Life has its challenges, but it is how you deal with those challenges that shape you into who you can ultimately become.

Inspiration

Miracle. That is a word that can sum up the sixth round of chemotherapy fairly well. Up to this point in my treatment there was no medication that would keep me from throwing up. It seemed like everything that we tried either worked for a while, or didn't work at all. All that was about to change.

We showed up at the clinic for round six and everything was going normally. Rochelle accessed my port, and while she was doing that Nancy came in and told me that the pharmacist had an idea.

"We are hoping that we came up with the right combination of meds for you, Jonathan," she said. "Assuming you will make counts, we will give you three different medicines. I talked to your dad and one of your family friends suggested that you try a drug called *Emend* because it worked like a charm for her. It might sound like a lot of medicine but it will be worth it if it works. Sound good?"

I don't care if I have to take 50 pills as long as my nausea is under control. I nodded my head and told Nancy that I would like to give the combination a shot.

We waited in clinic for a while and throughout the process I ate several bags of Cheetos and Sun Chips. I talked to Jamie and Shelley and we laughed a little bit as well. I had become used to waiting to get up to the floor and gradually my patience improved. *It won't do any good to complain.* After several hours Jamie came in with a clipboard and told me it was time to go up to the floor. As we got in the elevator, Jamie asked me if I was excited to be finishing my first session of chemo.

"I am very happy and this weekend I will be working on homework, so that should keep me busy," I said.

I was always looking for things to occupy my time when I was getting chemo. I would talk to nurses, care assistants, doctors, patients, parents, and the custodians. I loved the atmosphere on the floor and it definitely helped to be active and not just sleep all day.

I was wheeled out of the elevator and once Jamie held her I.D. badge up to the decoder, we heard a *click* and the door opened.

"Alert the fan club," said R.J., laughing as I was wheeled down the hall to the right and into a room.

I talked for a few minutes with Rochelle, a spiky-haired nurse who commuted to work at Children's Mercy almost every weekend. She was also quite a jokester and we instantly got along great. She told me if I needed anything I could ring out and she would be there in an instant.

That night after I had taken the Emend, Kytril, and Decadron I felt all right until I started getting hiccups. These weren't normal hiccups either; they were the worst I had ever had. I called Rochelle and asked her if I could have anything for them.

"Hiccups, huh? Well there is a drug called Reglan that sometimes works on kids," she said. "I will order you some from the pharmacy if you'd like."

"I would really appreciate *~hiccup~* it."

By the time the Reglan was delivered, Rochelle had already given me Benadryl, and I was surprised I even had enough energy to hiccup.

After the Reglan, the difference was like night and day. Within a few minutes I stopped hiccupping, but my stomach was sore. I could barely open my eyes and finally I lulled off to sleep.

The next morning I was feeling more rested than I had the night before. I heard a knock on my door and Mandy came in with my meds.

"Look who's awake!" she said jokingly. "Can you take this (Emend) and these other three pills (Decadron) for me when you get the chance?"

I was feeling so much better that I picked up the medicine cup and the water that Jennie brought to me when I was asleep and I downed the pills.

"Are you working all weekend?" I asked.

"Lucky you, you will have me for two days and hopefully you will go home Sunday," she replied slyly.

"I am so bummed," I lied with a smile.

She gave one of her trademark Mandy giggles and then asked, "Do you need anything?"

"No I'm good, thanks. Do you need anything?"

"No I'm good," she said mockingly.

Right as Mandy was walking out of my room a physical therapist came into the room. I tried to bend my knee further and further during each admission for chemo. *I will be satisfied with my knee and try to make progress every time that I get it worked out.*

After PT was over, Jennie checked my blood pressure and my temperature. Both were normal and she sat down in a recliner beside my bed.

"How are you doing, handsome?"

"Doing pretty well," I said. "Just been reading through this book of notes and letters my friend put together for me."

"Who are the letters from?" she asked.

I showed her my book and she read a few of the entries.

"Jonathan, you have no idea how many lives you are touching each day," she said. "And not many kids have the support that you do. So many nurses and care assistants love having you as a patient because you are so kind and polite," she told me. "You are fighting the fight but you have an amazing attitude, too."

"Jennie, I have realized that I want to make as many lasting friendships here as I can," I said. "If people are trying to help me, the least I can do is try to help them by taking care of myself and being nice."

Not Alone

A guide may lead you,
But in a guide can you confide?
A crutch provides balance
But not a breathing being by your side.

One companion is enough
But why not carry two?
You can walk a little faster
Change a couple to a few.

A few will help you strive on,
They'll give kind words when you are weak.
Before you know how much they matter,
Followers join before you seek.

Some you'll have to ask
Most won't wait until you inquire
They know that times for you are perilous,
That your straits grow increasingly dire.

An abundance of forces mass,
Though differences they may possess
Your God is keeping watch on you,
You begin to worry less.

Quality over quantity
Is such a cliché phrase,
But if you have quality *and* quantity
A dark chasm becomes a simple maze.

A labyrinth might be big
Or it might be small,
But you'd rather have a way of getting out,
Then having no way at all.

And every time you turn your head
The masses seem to be
Stretching out like an army of love
That you can feel and see.

Not everyone can march,
Though their caring souls will send
Letters, prayers, and love abounding,
Until you find the end.

Stretching from Monterey to Baltimore,
Winnipeg to College Station
Spanning from England to Sydney,
Warm hearts' love flows with adoration.

Confidence is rising,
Realization hits you when you're shown
The numbers may be surprising
On this path
No matter when it's over
Just know you are not alone.

The rest of the day flew by and Saturday I slept in because of fatigue from the Methotrexate. A week ago I had new scans to determine what the status was for surgery. The realization it was then only a month away made me very happy.

On Saturday night I was trying to sleep, and when I got Benadryl I was out. I woke up about an hour later and was sweating like crazy. I buzzed for Rochelle after I woke up my mom and told her the sheets were soaked. Rochelle helped my mom change my sheets. All in all I figured that it was no big deal and I decided that I should go back to sleep.

About two hours later I woke up again. Rochelle came back in. After she changed the sheets again I fell asleep.

The next morning I talked to Mandy about why I had night sweats. She told me it was likely because of the steroid that I had been taking. I ate some breakfast and around 11:00 we got word from Mandy that my Methotrexate level was .01 (0.01 or lower to go home), so I was cleared to leave!

After I had taken the final meds, Mandy turned off the fluids and then got foam to de-access me.

"Do you want me to count to three?" she asked.

I always said "If you want to," so everyone usually did. She pulled out the first needle, and about 20 seconds later she pulled out the second one. She then put a cotton ball on my port and added a Band-Aid to stop the bleeding.

"I think I have a sore in my mouth," I said. "Could you please check?"

Mandy looked in my mouth and saw the same white spot I had seen.

"I really hope I don't get mouth sores."

Mandy looked at me sympathetically and said, "All you can do is take care of your mouth with good hygiene. Maybe you won't get them this time."

We left the floor and Mandy pushed our cart out to the parking lot. We were parked on the first floor and we put our entire luggage into the trunk. After it was shut, Mandy gave my mom a hug and then she came up to me and did the same.

"We are going to miss you but I know it will be nice for you to be home for a while," she said. "I bet you are excited to have a break from the hospital. Good luck with your surgery, dude!"

As we drove away I thought to myself, *I am happy to have a break from chemo, but I'm not necessarily happy to leave everyone on the floor.* I realized, however, that there is a time for everything.

Six rounds were out of the way and I knew I had found a second home on 4 Henson. This was God's plan unfurling before my eyes. I can't begin to express my thanks to Mrs. Stark for suggesting Emend— this made all the difference in getting through chemotherapy!

Chapter 10: Journey

Dedicated to: The Pigeon on a Hill

Countless pigeons sat outside the windows of every room I stayed in on Floor 4 Henson. My parents always commented about how those "those things were everywhere!"

No question, there were a lot of birds which took refuge on ledges on the opposite side of the glass. In the hospital, sometimes I would get to the point where I would stare at certain things for a prolonged amount of time. There was only so much I could look at while going through the individual rounds of chemotherapy. On a couple of different occasions I recall staring out the window minute after minute, sometimes slowly turning into hours.

What I realized about these birds was they were not safe from things I was protected from inside my room. What if the weather was harsh? Or what if one of them slipped off the edge and couldn't fly? I started making comparisons to the position the pigeons were in and the position I was in. My immune system was down and it was much easier for me to have illness that most kids my age could fight off. I was being supported by so many, but in a way, everyone who loved me could only do so much because I was the one physically going through the treatments. I knew God was the one keeping me safely on the ledge.

Journey

When I got home from the hospital, I had something else that made me excited besides being finished with chemo for six weeks: the Pro Bowl. I am a huge football fan and even as unexciting as the Pro Bowl may be, I watched the sport whenever I could. The game had already started by the time we got home. When one of the announcers mentioned someone's fight with cancer, it instantly reminded me of when I had watched the Jimmy V. Classic in November.

Before one of the games, ESPN announcer Dick Vitale got very emotional when he described how much the Jimmy V. Classic had raised for cancer research over the years. A toddler who got diagnosed with a tumor in her knee told her parents one day that her leg hurt. Each day she said the pain would get worse and worse, and eventually when the family thought they should take her to the doctor, they did. They discovered a malignant tumor, but it was too late. The little girl died shortly after their visit. *That little girl was only four or five and her life was gone in a matter of weeks because they found out she had cancer too late.*

The moment I heard that story, my eyes filled with tears, and although I didn't make a sound, my face and my trembling body said it all.

"How do we know that I won't end up like that girl? What if I die because the chemotherapy doesn't work?"

I asked my parents. I asked myself. I asked God.

The word *if* is used hypothetically, but when I use the word *will*, I intended it to be used when I said, "I ***will beat*** cancer or I will cross that bridge of death *if* I get to it."

Speculating about the possible outcomes can have a big effect on the mental outlook of people fighting a terminal disease. Sometimes I would get excited about the thought of getting through treatment, and other times it felt like the road was too long.

There are three things you can do when you get cancer:

1.) Pray — Every day
2.) Hope — Look at everything as positively as you can, and wish for the best
3.) Follow — Listen to professionals and your parents or guardians and do everything you can to increase your comfort level and stay healthy.

Because your life can be taken from you at any moment (not just if you have cancer), you have to enjoy the simple things.

I realized if I was distracted by something I enjoyed doing, time went by faster and the cancer couldn't affect me as much.

I got a sandwich from Planet Sub to eat while I watched the Pro Bowl. I felt the white mouth sore on my gums, but my initial reaction was not to worry, but rather to try and forget about it. I watched the Pro Bowl and brushed my teeth thoroughly afterwards. Good personal hygiene was the best weapon to preventing mouth sores. I tried not to eat foods that would require intense brushing. I figured out that if I flossed my gums would bleed. If that happened, the blood could mix with the germs in my saliva and cause the bacteria to spread (sounds kind of weird I know). After every meal I would brush my teeth and use an orange-like sticky substance called Nystatin.

One thing that changed over break was the fact that the tutors came over three times a week. Ms. Burkhardt (U.S. History and English) came on Wednesdays and Ms. Hart (Math) would come for an hour on Mondays and Tuesdays. School was not necessarily hard to keep up with, but it also wasn't easy. I would get worn out quickly trying to "get everything finished at once." I don't like to procrastinate because I don't like it when stress comes into my life. I really don't want any more of it.

During the break, I had the chance to talk with many friends on the phone. I would often talk to some friends long into the night. I also kept in contact with many people through Facebook and texting. My dad made a sign that he put on the door of my room that read: "You did it! Part one completed with grace and courage! God is with you each step and so are we. We love you, Mom & Dad"

I couldn't help but wonder how many kids on my floor have parents who do something like that. Having this disease is hard, but how much harder would it be without a loving family?

Put on Love

The doctors and the medicine
Will always be around
The patients know they're in good hands
No matter what is found

Facilities can be topnotch
Food will somehow be consumed
There is something missing, though
When you are sitting in your room

Every kid has nurses
Care assistants are their aids
But do all the kids have loved ones
To call and visit them each day?

I love my parents, love my brothers,
Love my puppy, too
To complete your journey you can't go alone
Boats don't move without a crew.

One day when it's said and done
And my cells have no more cancer
I'll try to help kids who question
But never get an answer.

One has to find support somehow. One special source for me was Mr. David Pennington, who visited at the house one day. We had a conversation about my progress.

"How are you doing, Jonathan?"

"I cannot even tell you how thrilled I am right now, Mr. Pennington," I told him.

"The Lord has seen you through your first part of beating this thing," he said, smiling. "Can you believe how far you've come? It is really remarkable!"

"I have had excellent help, and God is the one who can wake me up and prepare me to face it each morning. I never thought I would say this, but I am fortunate God put me through this. I know He did it for a reason, and although I will try never to take anything for granted again."

Before he left, David asked if we could pray together. He weaved a wonderful prayer with his words, and gave me a fist bump before I crutched him to the door. He told me that his watch was set to go off in the morning, afternoon, and at night before he went to bed so that he could pray for me three times a day. It really meant a lot to me.

Later that day, my youth pastor, Kyle, came over and congratulated me for making it through the first six rounds.

"I am very relieved to have surgery soon," I told him. "The sooner I have the knee replacement, the sooner I can start physical therapy. The sooner I can start physical therapy, the sooner I can walk, and eventually run again."

"It has been a long road, hasn't it?" he asked.

"I have learned a lot along the way, but yes, it has been a long road," I said.

If there was anything I missed, it was the youth group. I will never forget when I got a framed picture of everyone wearing the black doo-rags with gold footprints that said: "Stepping together."

Kyle had also come to visit during my sixth round of chemotherapy, and along with him he brought a long rollout paper with most of the people in our youth group's heads attached to traced bodies. My nurse and Kyle attempted to put the poster up in my room because there was more wall space than usual in the room I was in at the time. In the middle of the night when my mom was sleeping in my room and I had been awake for only a few minutes, the rollout sign of my youth group fell. It made a loud noise that woke up mom and scared her a little bit, and I couldn't help but laugh when she asked what had happened.

"I guess you didn't see the rollout sign that was taped to the wall."

Some of the remaining days passed so slowly by, almost like the water droplets of a sink that hasn't been turned off all the way. Others sped by like currents that were swift and strong enough to cause floods. Fast or slow, I thought about two things: Making the most of the time, and my surgery on February 28.

We went in to see Dr. Rosenthal so that he could give me a brief run-down of what exactly he would be doing.

"Basically, the limb-salvage surgery will take anywhere from five to six hours. We have found a better way to do the procedure so you will heal faster and go longer without having your next knee replacement. If everything goes smoothly, which we anticipate it will, you hopefully shouldn't need another one of these for at least 20 years."

Limb-salvage surgery was the God-sent alternative to amputation. Dr. Rosenthal asked one of his assistants to grab an example of the kind of knee joint they were going to put in my right leg. The assistant handed it to Dr. Rosenthal and told me this would be similar to the prosthesis I would receive.

"Do you have any questions?" he asked.

"I have two questions," I said. "The first is, will I be able to see the prosthesis before my surgery? The second question is, what sports can I play after I have recovered?"

"Two great questions! The answer to the first one is no, because the prosthesis is kept sealed and sterile before the operation. The risk of infection is too great. However, I can have Kim take pictures during the surgery that we can put on a disc for you."

"So can I still run?"

"Yes, the main goal of having this new knee is that you can go back to doing as many things as you can normally. But the process to get them back is fairly painful and takes a lot of dedication. Some kids don't do physical therapy after knee replacement surgery because it hurts, and then they end up not being able to bend their legs past a certain point. There is only a temporary window in which you have to go from hardly any bend at all to 110 degrees, which is the optimum goal for where you want to end up."

"Can I play basketball for fun, tennis occasionally, or run to keep in shape?"

"I'll give you an analogy," Dr. Rosenthal said with a smile. "Your leg is going to be like a nice vintage car that you only drive a couple of times a week. The less intensely you use it, the longer it will be before your next knee replacement. If you were to drive a nice car from the seventies around every day, you would slowly break it down. For all of the effort you will put in during physical therapy, the less harm you will want to do to your knee, trust me."

Dr. Rosenthal had a pretty good sense of humor, so he decided to give me something to think about.

"You know, I know a lot of guys that are my age or older that are thinking about having knee replacement surgeries, and you will have a leg up on them because you are only 17. Your advantage is that you are young and you are in good shape. Not to mention you have a desire to be off crutches, which you could be off of in early summer if you work hard."

I thought about what Dr. Rosenthal said as we got ready to walk out of his office. *I am doing something now that most people don't have done until their forties, fifties, or sixties. I am lucky to be in good shape and I am blessed to have one of the best orthopedic surgeons in the Midwest to do my surgery.*

I decided if I could get through chemotherapy, then I could get through this operation.

Chapter 11: King of Kings

Dedicated to: Jesus Christ, my Lord and Savior

There is only one person in this world that I love more than my parents, and His name is Jesus Christ. There is only one dedication in this book that truly needs no explanation, and this is it.

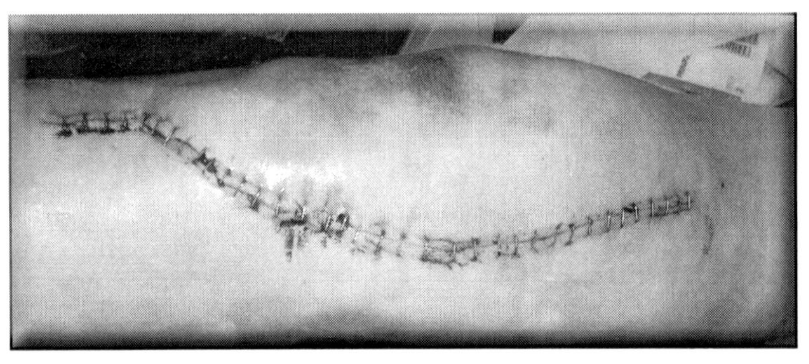

King of Kings

February 28, 2008 is a day that I will never forget. That day is the one where I got a foot-long scar as a souvenir from my fight with cancer.

I did not eat anything the night before the operation. I knew that this was the biggest surgery I would have and I prayed with my parents that everything would go smoothly. My motivation was that I wanted to walk again, and that was all I needed.

Dr. Rosenthal came into my pre-op room and made marks with a pen on my right leg where the surgery would be performed. The nurse then shaved my leg in that particular area and I waited for the anesthesiologist.

He walked in and asked me my name, what my birthday was, and what my surgery was for.

"Jonathan Stepp, March 9, 1991. I am having limb-salvage surgery on my right knee."

"I am glad you know what's going on," he said with a laugh. "I will be administering some anesthetic that is going to put you right to sleep. It might sting for a few seconds but then it will be no big deal. We will also put a catheter in so that you won't have to worry about getting up and going to the bathroom. We will also put a blood drain line in for your leg. Sound OK? Any questions?"

Dr. Rosenthal came in and he shook my hand. As I looked at him, thoughts began running through my head. *Dr. Rosenthal is the best orthopedic surgeon around and I am going to be fine. He has done hundreds of surgeries before, so what do I have to worry about?*

"The surgery will last for about five hours," he said. "Once you wake up we will use a CPM (Continuous Passive Movement) machine to start moving your leg and get some circulation back. Don't worry, it is very gentle and although you might be uncomfortable, it should not be at all painful. We will also get you started on crutches after we take out the catheter."

"Is there any way I could get pictures of the surgery?" I asked again.

Dr. Rosenthal looked at Kim and she nodded her head.

"I can take them and then copy them onto a CD for you," she said.

Before my surgery one of my friend's moms came into my waiting room and wished me good luck. She worked as a nurse in the hospital, and she also told me that she would be in the recovery unit after the surgery.

As my mom began to pray for me, the Lord's Prayer popped into my head and I recited it. Then, while listening to my mom, I said in my head: *God, please watch over me. Help the doctors and nurses know exactly what to do. I pray that the pain isn't too severe and that I can start recovering healthily after the surgery. In Your Name I pray, Amen.*

The anesthesiologist came in with a syringe and an IV pole. I calmly watched him tie a band around my arm and stick me with a needle. I felt the medicine swim into my vein and I let out a little grunt. I then saw him take the needle from my arm as he put in an IV in and taped it.

"Great job. You're all set, kiddo," said the anesthesiologist.

He also said a nurse would be in shortly to take me to the O.R. My parents were encouraging but nervous. Their faces held mixed emotions, but they gave me a kiss and said, "You'll do great, buddy."

Several nurses came in and pushed my bed into the hall and toward the set of double doors that read: "Operating Room." One of them covered me with a blanket and held up a mask for me to breathe into. Gradually my eyes got heavy and shut. When I opened them again I was in the recovery area. I cannot ever remember feeling as good as I did. I could've fallen right back to sleep.

"Dr. Rosenthal said that it went great," my dad said when they entered the room.

"We are so proud of you," mom said.

I gradually fell back to sleep and I woke up when I felt my bed being moved. When I got up to the room things changed. My leg started to throb. The anesthetic was starting to wear off because the surgery had taken an hour longer than expected. I told my parents that I needed something to combat the pain. We called the nurse and she told me some medicine was on the way.

First I started to hyperventilate, then shake, and eventually I was writhing in pain. My right leg had been cut open, but it felt like it was still bleeding. I could barely move my upper body for what seemed like an hour (everything seems longer when you are in pain). I couldn't eat anything and when I tried to I threw up. The nurses and my dad told me that the next couple of days would be the hardest to get through by far. I fell asleep and Dr. Rosenthal came in later that night to see how everything was going. He told me that the operation went well and that recovery would be hard work but that I could do it.

The next day I woke up and started crying because the pain had heightened to its greatest peak. I continued to pray throughout my stint at Menorah. Each day the pain got a little more bearable and I had already become more comfortable using the CPM machine. I got the catheter out and after that things were looking up. I had very nice nurses and I started some physical therapy. My leg was wrapped in a huge layer of white bandages covering a brown wrap.

I looked at my leg and thought to myself: *This is a miracle. Ten years ago the only option would have been to amputate my leg from the hip down. Only ten years ago! Look at how far they have come.* This miracle reminded me of the Bible story with Moses rescuing his people from the Pharaoh in Egypt. God gave the Israelites delivery from Egypt. God's grace is why those people were saved. God's grace is why I am saved, even though I'm a sinner.

In the past I had thought about Jesus dying on the cross and how horrible it must have been. *Nothing you will go through in your life will be nearly as terrible as what He went through.*

True Heroes

Everyone has heroes
In movies, books and TV
These figures are much too strong
For evil foes to defeat

They will be remembered
As legends not forgotten
The bad guys never come out on top
They'll be picked apart like cotton.

But when you're searching for a great one,
Don't glorify a mask or cape
Look at what they do for those of us
Whose lives are out of shape.

Does your hero make sacrifices?
Will they help one through a loss?
Maybe you've heard of the man who died for me,
My hero was nailed upon a cross.

My hero was not an action figure you could buy in a store or a sports player you could get an autograph from. My hero was someone who I asked to come into my heart during elementary school all those years ago. My hero is still with me today, and He is never going to leave me.

Chapter 12: Love

Dedicated to: My dog, Dylan

Prayers, meals, support, letters, and kindness are all acts of love that I had been blessed with in the last nine months. Another source of love in my life has a furry white body, a fluffy tail, and a warm tongue. God sent me this source of love in the fourth grade, and he has never left my side since. I am talking about our dog, Dylan. He can make me smile when I am down in the dumps. He can make me laugh when I have had a stressful day, and he loves me no matter what. This is the kind of love all people should exhibit in everyday life, an unconditional love that shouldn't be held back. Dylan might not be able to talk, but that doesn't mean he doesn't have a heart. Dylan would sleep on my bed or keep me company, and he defined the term *companion.* I could count on him through thick and thin, and he never let me down.

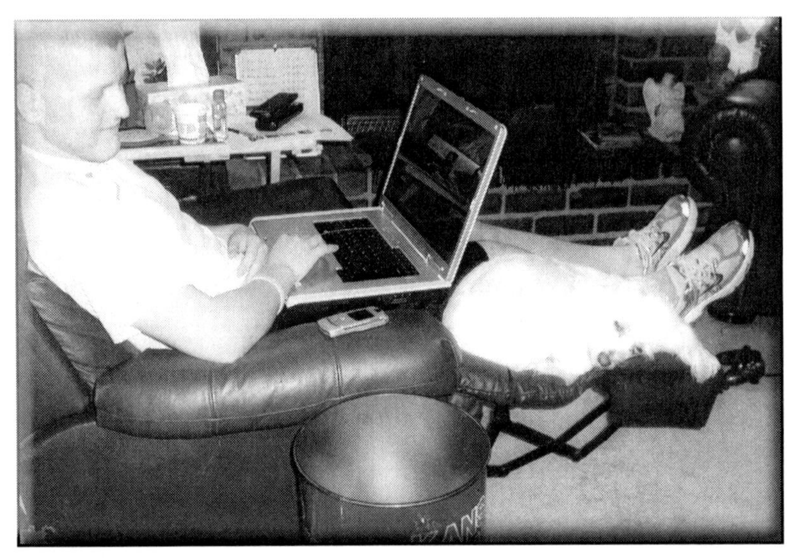

Love

By this point, I had gone through six rounds of chemotherapy and three surgeries. Things seemed to get a little better each day. My stamina was ever improving and bit-by-bit my hair was beginning to grow back. March Madness, the most exciting part of the college basketball season, was approaching, and this meant the Big XII Tournament was starting. I love watching almost all of sports, but none can compare to college basketball. I had enough time on my hands to watch virtually every game that year, and that was something I wanted to take full advantage of. KU had a bye in the first round of the tournament so I watched the other teams play. During one game, the announcers began to discuss Jimmy Valvano, the North Carolina State coach who in 1993 gave one of the most inspiring speeches I have ever heard at the ESPY Awards. One of the most famous excerpts is:

"I urge all of you to enjoy your life, the precious moments you have to spend each day with some laughter and thought, to get your emotions going. If you laugh, you think, you cry, that's a full day. That's a heck of a day. You do that seven days a week; you're going to have something special."

His speech, which I first heard a couple of years ago, placed my life into perspective. I had learned that each and every moment I spent on this earth was important because once it is gone, you cannot get it back. Many people do not appreciate that until their time is almost finished. Even people who don't have disease or disability could be silenced at any time.

Every moment matters. Even though I wanted the time to pass, I knew I couldn't just keep looking forward. *If I keep worrying about tomorrow all the time I will forget about today.*

One day I looked forward to, however, was my birthday. March is my favorite time of the year because of college basketball, school nearing the end of session, and my birthday (which happens to fall just before Spring Break). If there was one day in my time off that I enjoyed the most, it was by far March 9. Seventeen is an age that is in between two big age-marks. When you turn 16, you can drive a car by yourself all the time. Eighteen is when you can vote and check out puppies at Land of Paws with a parent. This made 17 my last official year as a kid. This would also be the year I would defeat the greatest challenge that I have faced.

My birthday was on a Sunday, and that held significance because of a previous Sunday birthday I had experienced. In 2003, I had my birthday celebration on the same day as when I was baptized. At the celebration luncheon afterwards, almost everyone came up to me and gave me words of affirmation.

"Jonathan, this is the biggest decision you will ever make."

"Jonathan, we are so proud of you and your choice to follow Christ!"

"Your walk with the Lord is not going to be easy, but with Him, nothing is impossible."

Every day since then I have had that belief. *Nothing is impossible.*

My Choice

Integrity is something
That few can really grasp
If your morals are feeble
What's to keep you from sin's clasp?

Two paths were shown
One attractive and one right
I heard shouting voices
But only one stood out with might.

It is said that a man who is strong in stature
Can move boulders heavy and small
Yet a man who is strong in faith
Can move mountains great and tall.

This Sunday: March 9, 2008, was a day I would never forget. In the early evening I had the opportunity to go to youth group and see a lot of friends. I saw Kyle, my youth pastor, and some of the other leaders as well. They had a big cake for me and I got to catch up with a number of people. I hadn't been this happy in so long and each and every person that was healthy came up to me and gave me a hug.

After I said my goodbyes to the youth group, I went and had a birthday dinner at Johnny Cascone's, one of my favorite Italian restaurants. Two of my friends, Owen and Regan, came along to help celebrate. They play live music there and it always has a neat atmosphere. For dessert I had their cheesecake because I always save room. Everything tasted delicious and I was fortunate to be able to eat because I didn't have mouth sores or nausea. I thought my stomach was going to explode afterwards but luckily it didn't! As we walked to the car I noticed what a beautiful night it was. The stars were out and it was almost as though God had planned it to be perfect.

I crutched into the door and saw my dog, Dylan, curled up in a ball on his bed. He instantly sprang up and stretched. He let me pick him up and I took him into our family room. I get fairly immature when I am with my dog and I treat him like a baby, even though he is 8 or 9 years old. I sat in our recliner and began to pet him and he licked my hand. Dogs are a great thing to have because they don't judge you, they don't ignore you, and they always seem to be there for you. Dylan was good at keeping me warm, keeping me company, and most importantly, keeping me happy.

Just before going to the hospital after the knee replacement operation, the final pathology report came back.

"There were no cancer cells in the bone! Congratulations!!" my mom and dad said at the same time.

At that time I let out the biggest sigh of relief I had ever made. I was stunned. Shocked. Excited. *I have twelve rounds of chemo left to go and I am cancer free? How?* My body must have been relieved as well because I felt pain-free. My knee was forgotten even though I had just had surgery a little over a week ago. Things like pain don't matter when you hear the greatest news of your life.

As stunned as I was, I had to get the word out. I sent a text to nearly everyone in my contact list and posted that there were no cancer cells in my leg on Facebook. Almost instantaneously people posted things like "Amen!" and "Hallelujah!" Some said they would just start crying. I couldn't cry, though. I could only pray and thank God for the day.

All the hours waiting, the nausea, and the mouth sores had been worth it. I felt like a new person. I could now fully understand how much I had been blessed. The schedule for chemotherapy was set, and barring any delays, I would be finished in late July. I had so much to look forward to and all I could do was smile. You have to have faith in God.

"The Lord is my Shepherd; I shall not want.
He maketh me to lie down in green pastures:
He leadeth me beside the still waters.
He restoreth my soul:
He leadeth me in the paths of righteousness for His name' sake.
Yea, though I walk through the valley of the shadow of death,
I will fear no evil: For thou art with me;
Thy rod and thy staff, they comfort me.
Thou preparest a table before me in the presence of mine enemies;
Thou annointest my head with oil; My cup runneth over.
Surely goodness and mercy shall follow me all the days of my life,
and I will dwell in the House of the Lord forever." - Psalm 23

You have to have faith in your doctors and nurses. You have to have faith in yourself. God was present and working. I had Osteogenic Sarcoma, but Osteogenic Sarcoma did not have me. I was ready to continue the treatments.

Chapter 13: Music

Dedicated to: Mr. Resseguie, former Choir Director

The number of times I have listened to music to make me feel better are immeasurable. Music can make you dance on the inside even when you cannot dream of doing it in person. Tracy Resseguie was one of the most compassionate people I have ever met, and he made my first three years of high school a blast. Rarely do you find a teacher who can discipline students and teach extremely well at the same time. I did not make it into Chambers Choir my junior year, but he told me to keep trying hard and never give up. Musicals, choir concerts, and the performing with friends are all things that I will forever cherish. One thing I will always remember is his saying: “Sing from your soul and you’ll never be wrong.” Mr. Resseguie’s dedication made our high school choir one of the finest in the state. Thanks, coach!

Music

Although I longed for it to, spring had not yet arrived. In a few days I would return to Children's Mercy Hospital for the first time in six weeks. I had received all I had asked for in my days off, and I was ready to re-enter the ring. My spirits were up and my body felt better than it had since I started chemo. I knew the fatigue would come back but I also knew that I could handle it. Every day I prayed for guidance and I tried my hardest to be productive.

One day I was busy reading the newspaper (the sports section, of course), and I saw several cars drive down my street and park on our curb. I saw right away that the group was made up of some junior and senior choir boys. They were carrying a bag and a bald man with a red beard was leading them through our yard and up to the front door. This man was Mr. Resseguie, my choir director. When the doorbell rang, I crutched over to the front hallway and slowly opened the door. Thomas, our choir president, and Mr. Resseguie were standing there. Everyone looked very excited and they gave me high-fives and handshakes after I got a big hug from Mr. Resseguie.

We all came into our living room and took a seat.

"You've been a trooper bud; I can't even tell you how proud we are of you. We miss you in choir and everybody would love to see you," Mr. Resseguie said.

"I definitely miss everyone, too," I said. "That has been the hardest part of this whole process: Being away from all of my friends at school. I miss singing so much."

I had not been to choir class in almost four months. I had not sung very much but I listened to my iPod a lot.

The four boys gave me the bag that they brought in and my face lit up.

"What is this? You didn't have to get me anything," I said with confused laughter.

"Open it," Mr. Resseguie said with a grin.

I reached my hand in the bag slowly and I pulled out an object that I had seen advertised but never touched. The object from the bag was a PSP! A PlayStation Portable!

"Everyone pitched in and we went out and got you something that we thought you could use to pass the time with."

I reached in the bag again because I saw something else. I pulled out a case, a memory card, and two games. They also handed me a card that was signed by almost everyone in choir.

"Thank you so much! You shouldn't have but I will enjoy using this!"

"The reason we got you a PSP is because you can play games, watch movies, and listen to music," Thomas said. "You can also use the Internet."

"Wow, I can't believe you guys did this for me…"

"You are part of our family Jonathan, and we wanted to show our support for you."

We talked for a few more minutes about how choir was going and they asked me if I was going to try out for Chambers again.

"Yes, I am going to but when is the tryout?"

"It's coming up in April," Mr. Resseguie said.

Chambers had been one of those things I had wanted to get into so badly and if I made it, I would reach my highest goal in choir. I had tried out the year before but I did not make it in. It really worked out for the best though, because I would not have been able to take part for half of the year. It was a blessing in disguise.

"When do you go back in for chemo?" asked Mr. Resseguie.

"I go back in on Thursday," I said.

"Well we will be praying for you and I will give the choir an update on how you are doing," said Mr. Resseguie.

I slowly got up and gave everyone a hug. Mr. Resseguie opened the front door and said that he would see me soon. I waved goodbye and went back to the chair I was sitting in. I started to think about all the people in choir who I missed seeing, and singing with.

When there was time to kill at home and I couldn't think of something to do, I would reminisce about happy memories. Our choir recorded my favorite two songs on the iPod during my sophomore year when we performed in New York. One was a five-movement requiem by Morten Lauridsen called "Lux Aeterna," which means "eternal light." It lasts about 35 minutes. The other was a piece written specifically for us called "Arise, Shine!" This was not just any song, this was a masterpiece. Mr. Resseguie has a friend named Dan Forrest who is a nationally known composer. He came to one of our choir concerts during my freshman year and listened to Choraliers sing a song called "Leonardo Dreams of His Flying Machine". This was the most difficult song we had ever heard performed. Mr. Forrest liked it so much he offered to write a piece just for Choraliers. He didn't ask for money, he just asked if we could sing it at Carnegie Hall. When we found out about the trip, a couple of kids almost fainted.

We flew to New York in February and sang at several locations, the most memorable of which was Ground Zero. That day, our choir was bundled up in the freezing weather but we all held hands and sang "O Nata Lux," one of the movements of "Lux Aeterna." There was construction going on behind us but it did not matter. As we were singing, people who were walking on the street far away started to walk over to listen. Individuals ceased staring at the names of the victims on the plaques and began to approach. When we were halfway through the song, the tears of my peers started running down their cheeks. After the music stopped, everyone turned to the person closest to them and embraced them. What a powerful thing: the gift of music.

Paint a Song

A song is a painting
Only sounding of beauty
Its aura majestic
So sweet to the sound

The notes are the colors
With which singers work wonders
To listen is fleeting
But its beauty abounds

Even not wonderful
Even not fine
One's singing can fill
The heart like a ration

One can be professional
And lack the enjoyment
But a song sounds the best
When it's sung with passion

You can belt your voice to the dawn
Or softly serenade the moon
Worry not how it flows
Life on earth is not long

Before time is gone
And you can't steady a tune
Sing from your soul
And you'll never be wrong.

Even if you don't think you sound good, you should sing if you love it. God didn't make us the way we are to be silent. You have to find your passion in life, and one of mine is music. If you pour your soul into something, you can reach your dreams. Music helped me get through tough times, and even provided me with the blessing of a whole other family I could rely on called choir. Mr. Foley, Shawnee Mission East's new choir teacher when I returned for my senior year, implemented a new phrase that showed selflessness amongst the choir family: "Many singers, one voice." The transition back to school was made easier with him at the helm, and I greatly appreciated the impact that he and Mr. Resseguie had on my life.

Music is one of the most beautiful expressions of the power of the power of God. In the words of Philippians 4:4, *"Keep on rejoicing in the Lord at all times. I will say it again: Keep on rejoicing!"*

Chapter 14: Nurses

Dedicated to: Mandy Symons

Being in the hospital for nine months is so much easier when you are around people who make you feel like you are at home. Floor 4 Henson became my home away from home because I was in the hands of God's angels: the nurses. The first time I was admitted onto the floor, I was taken care of by a nurse named Mandy. She had a great sense of humor, but she knew when she needed to be serious. I was sick for a number of days in a row, yet she would always cheer me up and make me feel better. At one point in the first six rounds of chemotherapy, the nutritionists told me I had to eat more because my weight was dropping dramatically. My parents tried to convince me to eat, but my mouth hurt so badly from the mouth sores. I couldn't chew or swallow without crying. It took a couple of talks with Mandy for me to finally start eating and drinking. She told me I was strong and she knew I could do it. Her support encouraged me so much. I have always had a close bond with her because she took such good care of me, especially during the toughest time.

(Mandy on left)

Nurses

Part of my head was covered with baby-soft hair as I ran through it with my hand. *Enjoy this while it lasts because you won't have it after today.* This day was the day I would start chemotherapy again. Whenever you have time off from chemotherapy, your immune system has a chance to re-boot and you don't worry about having to keep your head covered because of the cold.

Today might have been the best that I have ever felt going into the clinic. My parents and I arrived at about 8:30 and we waited to get called to the back. As we sat in the waiting room, I looked around at the families next to us and wondered how they were doing. There are always at least one or two adorable little toddlers running around, and today was no exception.

I was seventeen years old, so coping with something like cancer was a little bit easier than being three or four. At that age many kids tend to do really well on days when they get chemo, and they can just run around. It is so sad on the days when they are confined to their hospital beds and they don't feel like being themselves. At age 3 I was a crazy child. We still look back at home videos and crack up laughing because of the things that I did. *For many of these kids, there won't be a home video that shows them at this point in their life because they are spending most of their time here.* The nurses and staff just fall in love with the toddlers because when so many terrible things happen at the hospital, they need happiness and a little bit of comic relief.

Several times the door to the back part of the clinic opened and one by one the families disappeared. Eventually David the C.A. came out and said, "Mr. Jonathan, you can come on back!"

I smiled, got up from my chair and crutched back to the height/weight room. Shelley, the tall care assistant, gave me a big hug.

"It is so good to see kiddos with all that hair!"

The funny thing was that it had grown back white-blonde. I had gained a lot of weight, which was a good thing. At that point, David took me down the hall about two doors and Mary was waiting for me so she could access my port. She began to ask me all of the standard questions: What medicines are you on? Did you ever have nausea problems? Did you spike a fever? Did you have normal bowel movements? Did you have good energy?

We answered all of the questions and then she told us that Dr. Shore would be in shortly to talk about the next 12 rounds.

Dr. Shore smiled and kiddingly said, "I bet he is happy to be back here."

I smiled and shrugged.

"You've gotta do what you've gotta do," I said.

He pulled out the treatment chart and showed my parents what I had completed and what was left. We looked at the remaining schedule:

1: Cisplatin/Dox(orubicin)
2: Methotrexate
3: Methotrexate
4: Cisplatin/Dox
5: Methotrexate
6: Methotrexate

7: Dox
8: Methotrexate
9: Methotrexate
10: Dox
11: Methotrexate
12: Methotrexate

"I know it is hard, but if I were you, I would try not to look at it like you have twelve rounds left," said Dr. Shore.

Becky looked at me and said, "Look at how far you have come. I remember your E.R. visits and when you had to come back because you couldn't get the nausea under control."

I thought about those times as I smiled. My eyes watered but I immediately wiped them.

"Were there any highlights during your time off?" asked Dr. Shore.

Highlight? No. Just a miracle. I explained that I was on cloud nine when I heard that the pathology specimen was cancer-free.

Caring for a Cause

After everything they had done for me
And would continue weekly to do
Upon my heart was placed a chance
To give back and do good, too

The forms were sent out
To many families and more
In order to raise funds
For my hospital floor

Such a generous response
Was never predicted
When I checked the mail
Every day through our garage door

Generosity and kindness
Were never more clearly shown
Than when that cancer came into my life
And that sarcoma attacked my bone.

I wanted to try to do something to thank everyone on 4 Henson. How the fundraiser worked was simple. One day I talked to my parents about making a form that I could send out in order to raise money for the floor. Because of my love of college basketball, I called the fundraiser: "Bracketology for Oncology." People could donate at least $10 to Children's Mercy, and anything more would be awesome. People would write down who they thought would win the NCAA tournament and the ones who picked the right team would win a prize. At the end of the fundraiser I would donate the money raised to 4 Henson.

I couldn't wait until all the forms were in and the money was collected. We talked a little while longer and then they headed out the door. It was a long day because we had to wait a while to get up on the floor. We were greeted as we went past the desk on the left. People walking by would comment on my hair and the fact that I looked so healthy. It was so surreal going into my room with the white board saying, "Welcome back, Jonathan!!"

R.J. and a nursing student were taking care of me, and I was in one of the corner rooms on the floor. When I looked out

I could see the nurse's station and people coming from either direction of the hallway. I liked this location because it wasn't too quiet. I had a lot of energy so I wanted to be in a spot where I could talk to people.

I tried to look at the room assignment chart but it was a little too far away to read. Eventually my mom told me I should go walk around so I could stretch my leg and I crutched around the floor with her pushing my IV pole. I began to think about what the fundraiser was raising money for. I came to a conclusion: the nurses.

Angels in Scrubs

Comforting those who weep
Helping put little ones to sleep
These men and women
Who don the scrubs
Are there to show their patients love.

Not only do they do
Countless tasks before day is through
Mothers and fathers they become
When nobody is there
To nourish and care

If one believes that hanging meds
Along with changing sheets on beds
Is all that nurses daily perform
That person would be misled
Because nurses keep your spirit fed

What truly makes
A hospital floor a welcome place
Are not the warm beds and comfy rooms
It's knowing that in nurses' eyes
Your health means *everything.*

Why was the floor like a second home to me? Why did I cling to hope even when I looked badly and I felt sick? Who helped save my life? The angels in scrubs.

R.J. came back at 7:00 and told me that my nurse was going to hang the chemo. At that point I conked out for about an hour.

If that weekend had one bright spot, it was the fact that I got a good amount of sleep. I didn't throw up, and I knew I would only have to receive Cisplatin one more time. My leg was feeling better daily and I received a card from someone that had a bible verse: *Worship the Lord your God and his blessings will be on your food and water. I will take away sickness from among you.* - Exodus 24:25

That verse stayed with me for the next two weeks and I knew that I could make it through.

Chapter 15: Oncology

Dedicated to: Dr. Terrie Flatt

Before I had cancer, I was never really interested in medicine. Even though I am not going down that path, oncology has been a huge part of my life. One of the reasons why I was so interested was because of Dr. Flatt. This doctor always had a cheery attitude. We could have fun talking, but I was treated like an adult. If I had questions, Dr. Flatt always had answers, or would try to find them. It is hard to find someone who is as passionate about their work. During my stint at Children's Mercy I was taken care of by phenomenal doctors, and I have so much respect for this particular physician. Compassion is one of Dr. Flatt's greatest strengths, and I know God created special people like Terrie to work with cancer patients.

Oncology

Ballad of the Bald

My hair fell out
All systems down
Not gone
But down they were

Chemo wasn't my friend
But leave no doubt
Twas not an enemy
Just my cure

Science is noble
But you pay no heed
To the wonders
It can do

Until you're not
Just reading the medical magazines
Because the one that's fighting
Is you

It had been nearly three weeks to the day that I had been admitted to Children's Mercy for more chemotherapy. In the time I had off some very exciting things had happened.

The most memorable event was KU winning the National Championship.

Perhaps even better than just winning the NCAA Tournament was the fact that KU stomped North Carolina on the way. Even though he had left KU several years earlier, I still liked Roy Williams.

My mom's birthday was on the 16th, which was the day before I was admitted. We stayed home and watched a movie and a family friend brought dinner over to us. Brooke's birthday is the same day as my mom's, so as a surprise to her we brought a cookie cake to give her on the night of admission.

The day we came in there was a long wait in the clinic. Usually Thursdays weren't too bad but for some reason there were a lot of patients. We were placed in a room in the back of the hallway and to the right. I was feeling pretty good but had been stressing a little bit over homework that had been assigned on homebound.

Typically when we were in the clinic it was either a time to rest or a time to watch some TV and listen to music. I was looking forward to this admission because I was rested going into the weekend. Nancy had already come in and evaluated me. My blood counts were good and my ANC was high enough to receive Methotrexate. I cannot believe how much work goes into making medicine and coming up with the right quantity of chemotherapy to be administered. It takes some bright minds to figure those kinds of things out. I appreciated all the effort given on my behalf and for others with cancer.

At around 4:00 Jamie came into our room and told us there might be a bed opening up on the floor soon. She had my mom sign the form and we eagerly awaited her return. Thankfully about twenty minutes later she came back in and she was pushing a wheelchair.

Jamie used her badge and opened the door into the floor.

"Well look who it is," Mandy said as I turned and saw the nurse's station. "How have ya been dude?"

"I have been good, thanks. I haven't seen you in a while," I said.

"Yeah, no kidding! How have you been feeling?" Mandy replied.

"After surgery and my second to last round of Cisplatin, I am actually feeling very well."

"I am kind of busy, but I will try my hardest to stop by later."

"Sounds good. Thanks Nurse Mandy!" I said in a childish voice.

"Thanks Nurse Mandy!" she said back, humorously mocking the way I said it.

When I got to my room I saw that Joe Totta was my care assistant and I was really excited. He checked my height and then he brought in the scale and checked my weight.

Nick, the patient who I had met a while ago, knocked on my door and came in the room.

"Hey Jonathan how are you?" Nick said. "Hey Joe!"

"Hey Nick! How have you been?" I asked.

"I have been better, but have you seen Brooke yet? I have a birthday present for her."

He told me that his mom, who was an amazing quilter, had made Brooke a shawl. It was about 5:30 and we knew Brooke would probably get there in about 30 or 45 minutes. My mom put the cake next to my bed.

We looked at the clock after a while, and read 5:00, but no Brooke. Ten minutes later when the big hand moved to the 2, we looked again, but no Brooke. Finally, at 6:21 I saw a turquoise-vested, smiling woman with auburn-colored hair peek her head in the window. The minute she opened the door the glasses she was wearing almost flew off her face because my mom and Nick yelled "Surprise!"

I was just sitting on my bed laughing my head off.

"Whoa, that was a great surprise!" Brooke managed to get out.

"How was your birthday?" my mom asked.

"You know… it was pretty uneventful. But I had fun anyway. I feel like I'm getting old!"

My mom just scoffed and then she laughed. "Brooke you are way younger than I am. You don't want to know how old I turned yesterday…"

Nick gave Brooke his mom's shawl and she put it on.

"O my gosh I love it! Thank you and tell your mom thanks! Geez she is good!"

Later, Nick's mom came in to talk with us but first we brought the cake over and sang happy birthday.

We had a great time talking and Joe came in as we started cleaning up the crumbs.

"I heard a rumor that someone has cake?"

"You need a piece, Joe! We have some left!"

Everyone gathered together and we took a picture. My mom put it in my cancer scrapbook because it was a special night.

The rest of that weekend went very well. Now that I had meds that helped control my nausea, things were looking up. I got to go home on Sunday afternoon because they checked the Methotrexate level and it was below .1.

Memories last a lifetime, and it is important to enjoy the happy ones. After Brooke's birthday celebration I had the chance to rest and relax. The weekend was going to go well, and above all else, I was going to try and appreciate the little things. You have to try and search for joy in every situation, and then things look brighter even when times are dark.

Chapter 16: Prayer

Dedicated to: Heather Entrekin, former Senior Pastor at our church

Talking to God is one thing, but listening to God is entirely different. Listening takes patience, and when you aren't getting a concrete response or sign, it isn't always easy to wait for one. God works in mysterious ways and we don't always know why He does certain things. When I learned I had cancer, I blocked out my surroundings and prayed. I prayed He would give me strength and courage, and above all, wisdom. He told me my life would change, and thankfully He gave me the mentality that I would defeat cancer. My pastor Heather has drawn "prayer doodles" for me throughout the whole process. I don't even want to guess how long it took to create each doodle, because they are all so intricate. Every color in the rainbow and then some are used for them. Heather would just start with a Bible verse, and she would then start to draw pictures and write more words around those pictures. She claimed they just took time to make, but they were works of art in my opinion. Heather has shown me that with prayer, I can get through anything. God listens to everything I say, and now I have learned to listen to everything He says. Listening was also one of Heather's greatest strengths.

Prayer

It had been one of the longest seasons I have ever experienced, but winter was finally heading out the door. I could now go outside and not worry about putting on a cap to cover my head. This was a huge blessing. Now that the sun was beginning to show up daily, I had to take precautions to make sure that I didn't get burned. Sunscreen, one of my least favorite things to put on, was crucial. My skin was very sensitive, especially after the total knee surgery. My right leg was much darker than my left and it supposedly would stay like that for a whole year.

In my time off, which was roughly three days, I did some schoolwork and tried to relax. My mouth had some sores that were starting to appear even though I tried to be very diligent about practicing good oral hygiene. *The less sores the better, so keep brushing your teeth!* Coming up that weekend was the NFL Draft. This is an event I had to watch on TV every year because I love football. The draft would be on Saturday and Sunday, so I decided to invite Owen and Mr. Gray to the hospital to watch the beginning of the draft on Saturday. We pulled out of our house at around 8:15 and got to the hospital at around 8:35. We went to the clinic and Anna and Ryan were manning the check-in desk.

We waited in the front section of the clinic for a few minutes and then we got called back. We went into one of the rooms after I had been weighed and measured.

Rochelle came in and told us that the room situation was kind of a crapshoot.

"It is very full up there today, but we will try to get you a bed as soon as a spot opens up!"

It is amazing how much one event can change my life. I have so much more patience than I did at this time last year. Complaining about something I can't control is only going to stress me out. Not to mention it will probably stress everyone around me out. When I had an iPod, a PSP, and magazines to read, it usually wasn't that hard to pass the time. I would also talk to the care assistants and all of them were very entertaining.

At one point David came in and told some jokes after he made sure I didn't need anything. I could always count on him for laughter. The day continued and even though I didn't ask Rochelle, she updated me on the room situation pretty often. Eventually a room opened up at about 4:45 in the BMT.

The one big advantage to staying there was that it's very quiet on that part of the floor at all times. That was good because it was draft weekend.

At about 5:15 we headed up to the floor and made our way to the BMT. It had been a pretty long day and the first thing I did was turn on the TV. I was looking forward to Saturday so much. The cool thing that happened Friday afternoon when dad came back up to stay with me was that I got some mail. Some of it was in response to the fundraiser and I was excited. The other cool thing came in the form of a two-fold letter with a gold sticker taping it shut. It wasn't in an envelope; it was just folded and addressed to me from a church I had never heard of.

Love in an Envelope

From Nashville, Tennessee?
A letter sent to me?
Shaking my core
Had I met them before?
No, but that's what prayer does.

Next, a church in the middle of Kansas?
I try but I cannot understand this.
Brothers, sisters in Christ
Their love did entice
Yes it did, because that's what prayer does.

In their thoughts until chemo is finished
My hope can no longer diminish
God planted this seed
Heart, mind, and soul He will lead
You know why?
How? Because that's what prayer does.

Often my thoughts start to wonder
Why don't I tremble when I hear the thunder?
After all of these years
He has conquered my fears.
Yet He has, because that's what prayer did.

I will continue to fold
My hands in the mold
That so far has kept me afloat

And hear me, take note
I'm not alone on this boat

Through prayer
I am anchored in Christ.

The letter I received was from the "Prayer Room" of a church in Tennessee. We knew a family that had moved there named the Ryans who we kept in touch with. Odds are they told the church about my diagnosis and decided to write to tell me they were praying for me.

The encouragement you get when you know people are praying for you is substantial. The feeling you get when you find out people you don't know are praying for you is even better. It made me want to reach out to others because I was reached out to. When I pray, it is always calming and comforting. There is a certain feeling that is truly unparalleled. It is a way you can connect with people that live across the world, or people that live two blocks away from you. At that point, it was hard to comprehend how many people had sent me cards and how many different churches and support groups were praying for my treatment.

The weekend was going pretty well and that Friday gave me an opportunity to relax before the draft. My friend Tucker came over before the Grays did and she brought me McDonald's for breakfast. The Grays showed up just minutes before the draft actually started with Wendy's to eat. We watched and enjoyed each other's company. I watched the rest of the second round, even after Owen and Mr. Gray had left. Later Lynsey came in and I talked to her about the draft as well.

The next day I was discharged later than expected (around noon), but it didn't bother me. Before I left the floor, I thanked God that the weekend was so enjoyable. Things had gone very well and the fact that I now had mouth sores from the second consecutive week of Methotrexate didn't even bother me. I would be back up on the floor Thursday, and because it would be my last time receiving Cisplatin, you can bet it had been circled on my calendar for a long time.

Chapter 17: (Never) Quitting

Dedicated to: All Cancer Patients

Seventy-five percent of beating cancer is a mental challenge. The other twenty-five percent is the chemotherapy and medicines you take. Forging on gets easier when you can see the blinding bright light at the end of the tunnel, but it is hard to handle the initial shock that hits you when you find out you are another soldier in the fight against cancer. You didn't sign up for this. Why would God allow you to have cancer? For me, the answer to that question has been revealed. God gave me cancer to save my life. Yes, I used the word "save." We do not realize how precious life is until being close to losing it. Before I was diagnosed I thought I would never be presented with any health problems until I got older. I did not consider how blessed I was. I did not wake up every day and appreciate the little things. I have been given a whole new perspective and now every moment is a blessing because I am still alive. It took nine months, but I tried not to allow myself the opportunity to give up. Quitting was **not** an option.

(Never) Quitting

Summer fever had hit me like a brick. I was eagerly waiting for the day when I could have a break from homework. Physical therapy was starting up at the hospital in addition to using the CPM machine at home and in the hospital.

I really did not enjoy physical therapy. The importance of recovery was something I wouldn't really realize until much later, but I still tried to do everything I was supposed to do. My goal was to be off of crutches at some point during the summer. *If I work hard enough at something and believe, I know I can do it.* At the same time, my knee wasn't what you would call "loose." I could not bend it very much but I was told to start putting a little bit of weight on my right leg when I would walk around on crutches. At times, determination could be my greatest strength, and I was determined to get full range of motion back in my right leg.

I was still getting over mouth sores. They hadn't appeared all over my mouth, but they were definitely still there. Sometimes they would give headaches and I would take pain medication. The problem with taking the pills was that it could mess up your bowels. People often laugh about constipation, but it can be a serious problem.

This next round would be the last one for several weeks. I was looking forward to completing Cisplatin, and I would be a third of the way through the remaining chemo once I received it.

On Thursday, May 1, we went into the clinic and had blood counts checked. We found out that it was high enough to proceed with more treatment. I was already hooked up to an IV pole and just had to get fluids for most of the day. I got the chance to talk to David and Kaylynne for a little while in the clinic and took full advantage of anything that could help me pass the time.

If I was able to, I could talk to David for hours because he is a very interesting individual. He is an author, a poet, and he is very skilled at martial arts. He was a great listener, too, so we always had good conversations.

Kaylynne was a big KU fan and it was neat talking to her about the National Championship. I was watching TV and Matt, my psychologist, knocked on the door and came in.

Matt was a K-State grad and he remained a loyal fan. I delighted in reminding him that we won the Orange Bowl and the National Championship in the same year. With Matt, I tried to look at both sides of the KU-K-State rivalry. With Brooke, an avid Mizzou fan, there was only one side: Kansas.

For a good thirty minutes, Matt talked with me about how things were going and how excited I was for summer. He told me that if I didn't see him in the next couple of weeks, good luck with everything and that he would talk to me soon.

At around five David helped my parents transport my stuff up to the floor. We got up there and I was assigned to room 17. Lisa was my nurse and she told me an order was placed by Dr. Rosenthal to have a CPM machine in the room. When we got there, the machine had been placed on the bed and I slipped my leg into it. It felt kind of funny because I could barely fit on the bed with the CPM. My head was stretched back at the top of the bed.

"That thing looks like a torture device!" said Lisa when she came in to bump up my fluids.

Emily, my night nurse, came in to check my vital signs.

"It says that an hour before you get chemo you get Emend, IV Decadron, and IV Kytril?" she said.

"Yes ma'am," I replied. "How have you been?"

"I've been good thanks, just a little tired lately. One of my other patients is a teenager and they were crying because they were in pain. Hopefully the medicine I gave her will help, but she is scared."

Emily told me she would be back before long with the Benadryl and I thanked her.

"You know, I don't know how you do it sometimes, Jonathan," she said. "You always try to have a good attitude, and I have never heard you complain."

The Good Fight

Are you gonna give up?
Or are you gonna get by?
When you want to shed tears
Take a deep breath and sigh.

Complaining is useless
And I don't recommend
That you run and hide
Because your cancer isn't pretend

You stand tall and face it
You hold your head high
And stare the beast down
Right dead in the eye

Take each day slowly
Each hurdle you'll clear
Think good thoughts as you fly
And your fears disappear.

Have a mindset, you see
"I'll beat you,
You won't beat me."

I know it's not easy
Clench your fists with might
You are going to continue
You can fight the good fight.

When I got cancer, I didn't want to be viewed differently. I wanted people to treat me like everyone else. At the hospital I knew kids who were so afraid and so sick. *I am lucky that I have a great support system, great parents, and feel so blessed to know that I am getting through the treatments.*

I woke up the next morning and learned that Mandy was my nurse and Briana was my C.A.

I hadn't seen either of them yet so I pretended like I was asleep when the door opened. The curtain was closed so I didn't know which one of them it was. I waited for the curtain to open and then jumped to find the doctors standing at the doorway making their morning rounds.

"How are you feeling, Mr. Stepp?" asked Dr. Manalang.

"I am doing very well, thanks. I am really thankful for Emend."

I thanked the pharmacist, Ricky, for combining it with the other drugs. "I was so glad it worked," he said with a smile.

After Mandy adjusted my chemo and walked out the door almost like a changing of the guard, the physical therapist came in and asked, "Are you ready for some torture?"

"Yes," I replied.

"Let the games begin!" she said laughing.

My mom got up and told me she was going to go talk to dad. Mandy dropped off the water and stuck her tongue out at me. While she was walking out I returned the favor and yelled, "Thanks!"

When the therapist started bending my leg, it felt like someone trying to push over a small but still-rooted tree. It didn't give very much and she told me she was going to create a workout regimen for me. We went over the exercises she wanted me to do and I tried to remember how to do them all. Once she wrote them down for me I thanked her and she told me to have a good weekend.

The rest of the day consisted of crutching around the hall a little bit, getting chemo adjusted, and talking to people that came into my room. Dad couldn't come to see me because he had a very busy schedule that day. Mom stayed with me into the night and I went to bed at 12:30 a.m., which for me was relatively early.

On Saturday I had a couple of visitors stop by. Wendy, our sister church's youth pastor, came and brought food, and Owen came in the early evening. Briana was taking my vitals and when Owen walked in and I started laughing because he is probably a foot taller than she. She pretended to be emotionally hurt and said, "It's not my fault he's that tall!"

We were talking about something and Mandy walked in and noticed his "Go Big Red" Nebraska shirt.

"Well at least someone in here is smart!"

"Yeah, N for knowledge, right?" I teased

She and Owen both had the *"Did you really just say that?"* look on their faces. Priceless.

Owen tried a comeback by saying, "You know Nebraska has the highest graduation rate for athletes in the Big XII?"

"No, but I do know where to go if I can't find my corn in the grocery store."

Owen and Mandy started laughing and Mandy said, "That was really lame!"

She headed out for the night and Briana jokingly said, "Goodbye Jonathan! I will miss you until we see each other again tomorrow!"

Owen and I continued talking for a while and Emily came in and noticed my chemo bag of Doxorubicin was almost out.

"Only about thirty more minutes on this and then you will be finished," she said.

I was very excited because this meant that I would go home the next day. Owen told me he would talk to me soon and he headed out the door.

I only woke up twice that night and it was because the IV had to be adjusted. The next morning Briana was taking my vitals when the doctors came in.

"Are you feeling well?" Dr. Manalang asked.

"I am feeling wonderful," I said. "Honestly, this is the best initial feeling after getting Cisplatin that I have ever had."

"I know you will be upset, but we're sending you home."

Briana said, "Of course he's upset, he won't be with me!"

The doctors and I just laughed and Briana just winked with a grin.

Ten minutes later, Mandy unhooked IV lines from my port and said I was good to go.

“Don’t do anything crazy like you usually do,” she said. “Don’t party too hard.” She smiled and gave me a high five.

Cisplatin was down in the ring and out for the count. A huge weight was lifted off my shoulders, and if I had wings, I could have flown.

Chapter 18: Reflection

Dedicated to: David Overbaugh, Rest in Peace

Two months before I got diagnosed with cancer I went and visited my friend David at Children's Mercy Hospital. The experience of being in the hospital to visit a friend was pretty new. My whole life I had been blessed with very good health. I saw David dealing with Cystic Fibrosis and hoped that nothing that huge would ever happen to me. David showed me that you have to value every day that you have on this Earth. That was one of the things to pop into my head when I was told I had cancer. I am so lucky to have caught the tumor at a very early stage and I will never take my health for granted again.

David lived his life to the fullest despite having Cystic Fibrosis. No cure has been found, yet he was still brave. When having chemotherapy I stayed in the hospital a lot over a ten-month period. Until his lung transplants, he stayed there off and on since the day he was born.

David was one of the most fearless individuals I have ever met. I looked up to him because he only worried about what he could control and he was always nice to everyone he met. The maturity he had for someone his age blew me away. He knew what was important and what was petty. David Overbaugh has shown me great courage, he displayed steadfast perseverance, and he demonstrated to me that faith in God could go a long way. As long as I live I will never forget his strength and the love he had for everyone he knows. He passed away, and he will not be forgotten.

Reflection

Junior Year in Closing

I wasn't there
But the school bell rang
Loud and clear
I still could hear.

Classmates called
Giddy with glee
The only one truly thrilled
Was me

Strenuous work I had been doing
Strong Spring fever had been brewing
The sun was flooding over the trees
You'd walk outside and feel a breeze.

And so I should
Enjoy a while
The jubilant joy
Had made me smile
My happiness was hard to hide
My spirit had overflowed with pride
The next year schemed in perfect rhyme
Cause I would graduate on time

Summer break had officially begun! No more homebound teachers. No more homework.

My focus shifted to receiving physical therapy more often and having a little bit of fun. I would get to see my friends more often because they were all out of school. Going to the hospital would even be more enjoyable because when I got there I could just relax. I had said good-bye to Ms. Hart and Ms. Burkhardt, my nice homebound teachers.

Bring on Methotrexate. I am ready for it. It is nothing new to me and I want to get it over with.

Looking back I can remember the feeling of uncertainty before I knew the facts about the treatment for my cancer. *Am I going to be all right? Am I going to have to get radiation? How sick will I be?*

Thankfully, before I dove too deeply into those questions, I stopped and asked God to help me, and to be in control. As I have mentioned, that decision was critical. Listening to God, my parents, and the doctors and nurses helped me more than anything else.

On Thursday morning, May 22, I was on my way to the hospital for the beginning of another three-week treatment. Though chemotherapy used to be a scary word, now it was just as routine as brushing my teeth.

Children's Mercy Hospital had been great, and I was looking forward to seeing everyone. I missed my "family," and when I arrived in clinic, they let me know they missed me too.

As time moved forward, it didn't bother me as much that my life was in a nine-month hiatus from what I was used to. Being tired was something to adjust to, just like anything else that comes up. I wanted to get through the treatment as soon as possible, and that's all that mattered. It took about seven hours to get a bed up on the floor that day, and I didn't mind one bit.

Shelley helped us carry and push everything, and we made it up around 5:05 p.m. My dad put a tissue box on the rolling tray to the right of my bed. We put my IV pole on the left side of my bed as usual, because the port was on the left side of my chest. Two urinals went next to the IV pole. My mom set up her sleeping area on the couch. Manda, who was one of the nicest nurses you could meet, came in and checked my vital signs. She ran and got me something to eat and I had to go to the bathroom. She was already back by the time I grabbed my crutches. My parents went to the parent room because they knew that Brooke would be there soon, and I had to go to the bathroom anyway.

Once Jessica had taken my blood pressure she told me to page her if I needed anything. At around 6:10, I was out of bed and trying to grab my bag. Brooke knocked on the door and came in.

"What are you doing?" she asked.

"Getting my iPod," I said with a laugh.

"Need some help?" she said, a grin stretching across her face.

"Yes, please."

She went over to the rolling table and grabbed the bag. She handed it to me and said, "What's up? Where are your parents?"

"I actually told them that I would be OK by myself this weekend," I said.

She halfway believed me and said, "Oh, well who is staying with you?"

I pointed at the white board as if Manda and Jessica were, but the look of confusion on Brooke's face made me start to laugh.

As she gave me the eyes-rolled-up-whatever look, I got a call from my friend Holly, asking if she and my friend Regan could come visit me. The only problem was that they had gone to Children's Mercy's South by mistake. At the time I didn't know this but around 8:15, Brooke walked in with the two of them and said, "You have some visitors!"

Holly began by saying, "O my gosh J-Stepp I am so sorry that took so long!"

Regan looked at Holly and then at me and said, "We definitely thought that you were at the other Children's Mercy," with an embarrassed laugh.

I got the chance to visit with them for a good forty or forty-five minutes. They gave me big hugs because they had to head out and they told me "good luck." It had been great to be with them.

Overall, the weekend was a success because I got to go home at around 10:00 on Sunday morning. I was tired, but I could not have been happier that it was summer.

Chapter 19: Support

Dedicated to: Mr. Pennington, Cross Country Coach

The word "friend" is something that has a new meaning to me. I met a life-long friend, and that person is Mr. Pennington. During the day he will send me words of encouragement through texts, like: "Keep fighting, we are all rooting for you."

There have been countless times he has visited me and talked to me about how life is going. That means the world to me because he has been there the whole time lending a hand. I had the greatest support system to get through surgeries and chemotherapy. I cannot imagine facing cancer without having had this support. Cards, visitors, and people making food for my family have given me an incredible boost. Mr. Pennington would pray for me three times a day, and knowing that was such a blessing. So many people have been praying for me, and that is the greatest gift that anyone can give. Thank you, Mr. Pennington.

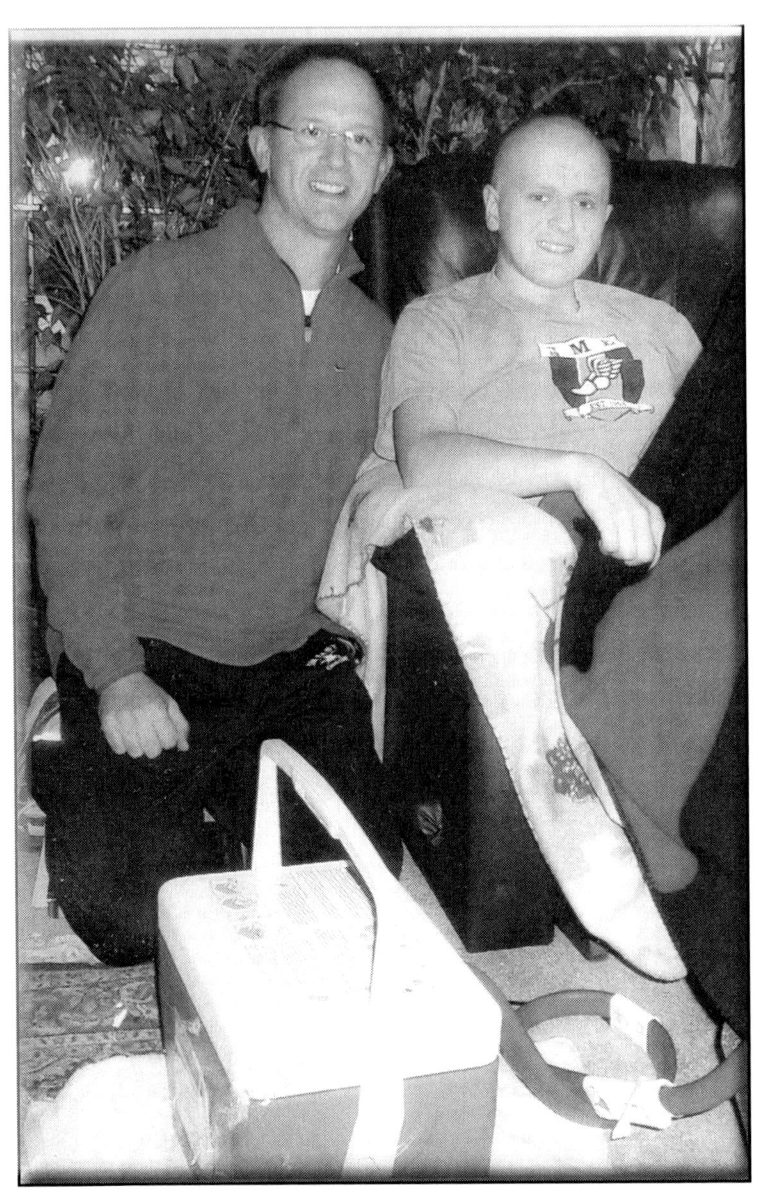

Support

In the middle of the night I woke up from a terrible dream. I was sweating and went to the sink to get some water after grabbing my crutches. My dream was twisted because I was at the hospital and I couldn't find my parents. Nobody had any idea where they were. I always had at least one of them with me at the hospital because they traded off. I got back in bed and thought about it.

I have two wonderful brothers, two incredible parents, and one adorable dog. I also have a network. A circle. A fellowship.

Certain people I could send text messages to, and certain people I could sit and visit with for hours. Others I could talk on the phone with for as long as I wanted. God put all of these individuals in my life for a purpose.

Round 6 was coming up and my mouth was feeling a little bit sore. Sleep was a little hard to come by. When I would take Benadryl, I'd either fall asleep and be out, or I would be up most of the night.

Heading into Thursday, it was the end of May, and I felt freer to stay up late. No more school meant that I could practically run on my own schedule. If I wanted to sit around and watch TV, that was OK.

The 29th arrived, and I had my stuff together the night before. Unfortunately I made the dumb mistake of staying up until 3:00 listening to music and reading a sports magazine. I was a zombie on the way to the hospital, and was so tired when I got out of the car that I thought I would throw up. I breathed in and out several times over the course of a few minutes. When I had the strength to get out of our mini-van we headed up to the hospital. When we got up to the clinic I had to be assisted into the room in the back where I had been going a lot recently.

Mary came in and asked if I felt nauseated.

"I think I'm just overly tired," I said. "I didn't get a lot of sleep this week."

Thankfully, I ended up making counts. We waited for awhile to get up to the floor, but not nearly as long as usual. Around 3:30 Jamie came in to have my parents sign the waiver form that said I could go up to the floor, and we headed right up.

The floor was in a fairly joyful state when I arrived. The nurses were laughing, and everyone looked happy. That was a good sign that the weekend would be pleasant (although I can honestly say that I never had a bad experience with the nurses, doctors, or care assistants on 4 Henson).

That afternoon one of the physical therapists came to my room and helped me.

"How is your knee feeling?" she asked.

"It feels all right," I said. "I can't say that I have had any pain, so that's good."

"Have you been doing your exercises?"

I probably haven't done as much exercising as she wants me to do, but it's not like I haven't done any. The exercises weren't fun but they also weren't that hard. *I just need to buckle down and do these.* Most of them worked on improving flexibility, but some of them involved me walking in the hall. The best way to make progress when you have a total knee surgery is to do everything they ask you to. It was a workout because I had a very low amount of stamina. My parents never wanted to be in the room when I did therapy because they didn't want to distract me and they knew I tried to follow the therapist's instructions.

I decided that I needed to get more reps in so we kept working. We finished about five minutes later because I felt exhausted and she had to leave for the day. God had pushed me through.

Later that night Brooke came in and we talked for a while. I was sitting on the bed and she asked me if I used anything to rub on my scar.

"Yeah, I use a certain kind of oil because it is supposed to make it fade," I said

"Do you have it with you?" she asked.

"Yeah," I said.

"I don't know how much it actually fades the scar though…"

She asked me if I knew how to apply it.

"Dr. Rosenthal taught me to rub it sideways firmly on the scar."

I got the bottle and used it. It tickled a little bit because the area around my knee was still kind of numb. This became a weekly task and bit-by-bit the scar eventually got a little less noticeable. Brooke told me that someone had to encourage me to do it. God had pushed me through.

The rest of the night was pretty quiet and I kept my lights on until mom came back. Dad was staying with me and he asked if I wanted to turn off one of the lights. I said I wanted it to be lit up for as long as possible. I liked to stay up late. I liked having the lights on, and I liked being in rooms with cool temperatures. I liked keeping the door opened a lot so that my room looked welcoming to visitors, nurses, doctors, and care assistants. On Friday I crutched around the halls all day and night. With one of my parents pushing the IV pole, I liked being out and about. My parents encouraged this because the more active I was, the better I would feel. I would be able to get exercise and I wouldn't have any constipation problems, either.

On Friday Linda Rix visited me. She was a jolly woman with red hair who was like a second mom to many people in the youth group. Linda was a nurse who belonged to our church and she was one of the youth group leaders. She was a great person to spend time with because she was a wonderful listener. If I wanted to listen, she would talk. She gave me lots of great insight and could talk with me about almost anything, while remaining very positive. She had been one of my nurses at Menorah when Dr. Rosenthal did the first surgery. That night we talked about life and how things happen for a reason. She encouraged me that I was strong enough to beat it and persevere.

Age with Wisdom

What doesn't kill you
Makes you stronger
This journey I'd endure
Would be worth it in the end
Because they found my cure.

Eager, worried, anxious:
Patients want healing with just a snap
But you can never reach point B
Unless you have patience and a map

Knowing where to go
Is important, it's true
Getting lost discourages
More than just a few

Lean on past experience
You might age more than you wish
But once you're done
Your problems
Won't matter
You will have happiness.

I was starting to feel pain in my mouth. It hurt but Linda and my nurse suggested soft foods. I sipped water and a milkshake and Linda made a list of ideas for what I could eat. After encouraging and persuading me, I ate some macaroni & cheese and had more water. My mouth ended up being sore later, but I had to stay hydrated and I had to keep my strength up. God had pushed me through.

Saturday was a great day because I had the chance to read and relax, and I was doing well with excreting the Methotrexate. I was going to the bathroom a lot, and I was feeling all right. When Sunday morning arrived, we checked the Methotrexate level early in the morning. At around 2 or 3, Emily, my night nurse, came in and drew labs.

"Hopefully you can go home later this morning!" she whispered.

About an hour later she came in and smiled.

"Congrats, you are going to be discharged!"

Like He had already done so many times, God had pushed me through...

Chapter 20: Trust

Dedicated to: God

Who can always catch me when I fall? Who is there to comfort me when times are tough? How did I know I would be able to beat cancer? I put my whole life in God's hands. Those hands have changed me into a new person. If you trust in Him, there is nothing you need to worry about. I have prayed before every surgery and every round of chemotherapy. Each time I have prayed, I have felt a sense of comfort and each time things have gone well. God has shown me that if I let go of the world and grab onto Him, He will lead me to the end of this journey. My Savior Jesus Christ died on a cross and He trusted God would resurrect him from the dead. If you ask the Lord to come into your heart, there is no such thing as death, only eternal life.

Trust

I was past the halfway point of the last part of treatment (12 rounds), and different problems surfaced that I had not experienced before. One of the "giants" that stood in front of me was the ongoing need for physical therapy. A wonderful woman named Sushma helped me. After stretching my right leg, she would help teach me exercises to regain flexibility. Repetition after repetition.

Work in Progress

Extension, extension
Working that knee
Making it better and stronger
That was the key

I kicked and I lifted
I lifted and kicked
Not a more tedious thing
In the world could be picked

Muscles were shaking
But I could not stop
The rule for PT
Is "Don't quit 'til ya drop."

Degrees of motion
Were rewards to attain
Working for 115 degrees
Requires ignoring some pain

I wondered and pondered
How long can this last?
But then I thought
I'm not trapped in a cast.

Looking at life
With a positive spin
All the while trusting in Him
Allows you to hold up your chin

One day I will be there
All the work will be done
And for old time's sake
I'll take a jog in the sun.

Sushma knew exactly what she was doing, because I would always come back in at the same level or gain some more ground. Her skill amazed me. Going through chemo at the same time as doing PT slowed down progress, and she knew how hard to push me.

"Tell me if I'm killing you, OK, Jonathan?"

"All right," I would say with a cautious laugh.

Physical therapy was doable because chemotherapy had become second nature. On the fifth of June I went in to the clinic, ready to do another round of Doxorubicin. The only problem was that after waiting longer than usual for the blood work to come back, we learned my counts weren't high enough. Doxorubicin was usually only a two-day round but I had a choice to make. *Do I sit and worry about being slightly off schedule for a week, or do I just give myself a week to heal and rest?* Option A would have been easier, but sometimes life isn't easy and I had enough experience to know that things would end up being OK. I chose Option B.

I had been so used to a pattern of getting things done that the week off was strange. I enjoyed having some extra sleep. At the hospital, there was no set schedule of when I ate or slept, just when I got medicine and chemo. At home I always was able to sleep, and I was guaranteed to have certain foods. Mom made me yogurt and fruit at least three times a day. Unfortunately I sat around more at home because I had my dad's laptop. Sports were more tempting to watch on TV now that school was out, too.

To my surprise, the week off went slower than I originally expected and I counted down the days until the twelfth would be here. The patience paid off when I had been in the clinic for a few hours on the day of my re-scheduled admit. I had made counts and my mouth felt better.

"Sometimes, people get a little off schedule, but that is completely normal," a nurse told me. "It is annoying to postpone chemo, but it might have been better for you to get some rest."

Now that I was at the hospital and preparing for another round, it really didn't matter anymore. *Play the cards you are dealt.* Mary had been in a couple of times to adjust my fluid intake, and now I was just awaiting the word from upstairs. The food delivery woman brought pizza, and I burned my mouth on the first bite. I was reaching for water when Shelley came in and told me that there was a room.

"Really?" I asked, perplexed.

The clock read 3:30 and I smiled. *This was the quickest times I have ever gotten an open bed!* Dad signed the form and we headed up. We saw several nurses and doctors on the way up and we said hi. Each person had a smile or a little bit of laughter as I smiled back.

On the elevator there was a mom with a little girl standing next to us. Before I put my mask on I looked at her and grinned. She was probably only three or four but she looked right back at me and laughed. Shelley commented, "Looks like somebody likes you!"

There were a couple of families walking in the halls with toddlers, but for the most part, it was a quiet day on the floor. I saw Brooke and we got to talk about how our lives were going. One hard part about being a patient was that people always wanted to hear about how I was doing. I didn't mind sharing, but I wanted to hear about how they were doing as well. Everyone was so kind and unselfish that sometimes all I would get to talk about was myself. I love talking to people, and I am more interested in hearing about what is going on in their lives. I was all too familiar with my own, and the attention was sometimes embarrassing.

That evening the Doxorubicin was hung and the infusion started. The chemical itself was red so all the nurses called it "Kool-Aid." When I excreted it, it would be red. The general consensus about Dox was that it wasn't as bad as Cisplatin. It made me tired like the other types of chemo, but it was only a two-day infusion. Then I would get to go home! You can't really have a "favorite" chemo, but if I had to pick, Dox would be it.

Friday night I stayed up late watching TV. Andrea was my nurse, a very nice brown-eyed, blond-haired woman in her mid-twenties. She *loved* her job. Several times she came in to adjust my infusion pump settings and I was wide-awake, watching an old western movie on AMC. She asked if I wanted the lights off and I nodded my head yes.

"Is there anything else you need right now?" she asked.

"Can I ask you a question?"

"Sure," she said.

She then sat down in one of the armchairs next to me in anticipation.

"What made you want to be a nurse?"

For about 10 minutes we had a deep conversation about how much she wanted to help people who were sick, specifically kids. She felt like it was her calling and she definitely had the heart for it.

The rest of the round went well and I ended up going home on Sunday morning. I was too tired to leave on Saturday night right after the infusion was complete. On Friday night, when I had talked to Andrea, I imagined a new door opening in my life. Maybe it had already been open, but I now noticed it. Why do people like Andrea become nurses and doctors? They have a heart that wants to reach out to children and tell them: "Don't be afraid of your disease, we are here to help."

Not everyone can appreciate how powerful something like that is. The first seventeen years of my life I didn't realize it. From the start I put my trust in the nurses and they poured every ounce of loving care they possessed into my treatment. God is always with us, but when He put nurses like Andrea in my life it was truly something special. I would just like to thank each of the wonderful nurses, care assistants and staff on 4 Henson at Children's Mercy Hospital.

Chapter 21: Unity

Dedicated to: Boz, my grandmother

As you grow older, lots of things around you change. Leaving your childhood is not an easy thing, and leaving the teenage years of your life is not easy either. One of the most constant things in my life was my grandmother, Barbara, who had the nickname "Boz." She was the matriarch of dad's family, and she was the glue that kept everyone strong. She defined many stages of my life by her acts of kindness and unwavering love, and during a tumultuous and unfamiliar time when I was dealing with the diagnosis, she was there. Sometimes all it would take for me to feel good was a simple smile, or one of her funny jokes. She was one of my favorite people in the world, and now she is with the Lord. She passed from liver cancer after a long fight, but she will always remain in my memories and in the depths of my heart. I love you and miss you.

Unity

Disappointment: a word that can mean everything, and a word that can mean nothing. At the end of my sophomore year, I tried out for Chambers choir at school and eagerly waited for the list to be posted. *I will be OK if I make it or if I don't, but I will be disappointed if I don't.* One afternoon I slowly walked down one of the ramps at school in order to check the paper. Mr. Resseguie posted it, gathered his things, and exited the premises to avoid being bombarded by students. Some kids had smiles illuminating their faces. I almost tiptoed my way to the door because I was so nervous. Once my eyes scanned the list my name was absent. Several of my friends' names were there and I didn't particularly want to talk to any of them yet. I probably looked like a zombie as I walked up the ramp. A couple of my friends noticed me and tried to talk to me.

"Remember, you always have next year."

I responded with a smile and a half-hearted, "Yeah, that is true."

That day I went home and called my voice teacher and told her the news.

"Jonathan, you can make that list," she said. "I really hope you decide to try out next year."

"I am not finished yet," I told her. "I will definitely try out again."

That was one of the hardest days of high school. The next few days in Men's Choir and Choraliers I was a shell. My choir teacher had told everyone that if they had any questions as to why we didn't make the list, we could talk to him at any time. I didn't think that there was anything that I had to say, so I didn't ask him any questions. He noticed, and the next week after he found out he came up to me in Choraliers and talked to me.

"You know Jonathan, you had a great audition," he said. "There is no question that you have a great voice. I hope that you will try out next year because you really have something."

If there was any more motivation needed, that was the spark plug. I took that information and thought about it.

Fast-forward a year and I find out through a text message that Mr. Resseguie is leaving for the brand-new Staley High School in North Kansas City. Kids were devastated. Some didn't want to be in choir the next year. It was especially hard for juniors who would be graduating the next year. On the outside, I kept my emotions in check because I knew that I could get through this.

Fast-forward to the upcoming eighth round of chemotherapy. When I got to the clinic I found out the absolute neutrophil count was at 241, which was too low to receive chemotherapy. I was slightly nauseous and the news was disappointing. *You can complain until you die, or you can suck it up and take another week off. Before you do anything, count your blessings.*

Giving into despair was not an option. When you have come this far, you don't let little things get to you. Sure, I would be off schedule, but once again, I hadn't been delayed that much overall, and I would make it into the next round after a week of down time.

When I found out I hadn't made Chambers my sophomore year, I knew I wasn't going to be discouraged. I worked harder than ever during the beginning of junior year, and every time I went to a voice lesson I tried my best to improve. In November I realized that even if I had made Chambers, I couldn't have done anything with the choir during second semester. Everything happens for a reason.

After I found out that Mr. Resseguie would not be there for my senior year, I talked with him and got a quick realization of how sad he was to be leaving. I knew he loved every single kid who came through our program at East. It was so hard to go to the year-end concert and realize that he wouldn't be there anymore. The performance was amazing, though, and I will forever cherish it.

When I tried out for Chambers in May, I was so excited just to be there. This was more than just a tryout that I had practiced for; it was about being with friends I considered as family. It had been five months since I had sung with Ms. Bliss, and when I went over to her house the day before the audition. She looked at me after our session and had a puzzled, happy look on her face. I was glad that she thought the rehearsal went well, but the next day a hurdle was placed in front of me before the audition: I had a bad cold. I didn't know how this would affect my voice, but I drank a bottle of water before singing. I was happy that the scales and solo went well. I prayed.

Dear God, please help me while I sing. This could be an incredible experience if I make it into Chambers, and it will make my senior year even more exciting! Please help me to remain focused and calm. Help my attitude to be positive no matter what happens. I pray all of these things in Your Name, Amen.

The last thing I had to do was sing my part of the school song. I thought that I did an adequate job, and after I finished singing, I was overwhelmed by the loving support of the choir. Mr. Resseguie gave me a patented bear hug and handed me the crutches. I left and called Owen on the phone to ask for a ride and he came and picked me up.

We ran over to Arby's so Owen could grab a bite to eat for him and his sister. Just then I got a call from Jonathan Harms, a fellow bass who had been in Chambers the past two years.

"Mr. Stepp, I heard a lot of auditions in there, but let me be the first to tell you, yours was amazing," he said. "I expected you to be there and try out, but I had no idea that you would sound so strong."

A rush of joy hit me, and I didn't know what to say. I just awkwardly laughed and told him "thank you" several times. We talked about life for a minute or two and he told me that would like to visit me soon in the hospital. I was excited and thanked him one more time before I saying goodbye. The next day I sat there and waited by dad's laptop. I kept hitting refresh because I was so eagerly awaiting the posting of the list. After a few minutes I went to the bathroom. I came back and went to another website to get my mind off of the posting. I heard a knock on my door while I was texting one of my friends, and I could hear my parents coming in. My mom was holding our dog in her hands and my dad had a piece of paper. They both had tears in their eyes when they set the piece of paper down on my bed. It was the list…

I don't know if it was just by pure coincidence or not, but the first name I saw was my own. I was in a state of shock. Under the "Bass" column, there it was.

The List

After the waiting begins
The suspense builds
You're in a strange mindset
And you get the chills

Working for three years
And then waiting two days
Ready to see
If a second failure would be my fate

Just ink on a listed page
That's all that it is
But if my name is in black
I will sing in happiness

I was thankful. So thankful. This was the choir I had aspired to be in since freshman year. It was an awesome group of singers and I couldn't wait until we would be together for the first time.

I was still facing a year without Mr. Resseguie, but everything happens for a reason. I looked at the week when a round of chemo was postponed in June, and realized how silly it was to be upset. I got to spend more time with both my parents and my dog, and that was a gift from God. *Be grateful for what you have, and know that even if things seem gloomy, there's always a silver lining in the clouds.*

Chapter 22: Visitors

Dedicated to: Brooke McGrath

Even on days where I was practically running on fumes, one thing would always perk me up: visitors. Some brought treats, some brought prayer, and some simply came to keep me company. I had been extremely privileged to have one special visitor every Thursday night when in the hospital. Brooke was almost like the equivalent of an older sister I have always wanted to have. She had a younger brother named Alex who would be my age today, but he passed away as a young child from a rare tumor. I met her in January 2008 and have enjoyed her company at Children's Mercy ever since. We developed a close connection and I value her friendship more than she will ever know. She would always bring me Lunchables and assorted snacks when I was hungry, and she made it a point to stay and talk for at least thirty minutes. It is not easy to come all the way downtown to visit, so when people make it down, I am always excited. Time goes by faster when you can look forward to having a visitor or two, but no visitor was more fun to spend time with than Brooke.

Visitors

One summer ago I had worked at a fireworks stand. Before my diagnosis, I anticipated I would be out at the fireworks stand again that summer. Priorities change when you are trying to finish chemotherapy.

On Thursday it was time for me to return and try to make counts again. I had prayed and hoped that I would be admitted to the floor. *As long as I am cleared to do chemotherapy, I will wait 12 hours to get up to the floor if I have to.* Rochelle asked us the standard evaluation questions when we got into a waiting room in the clinic. Anxiety kicked in. *Yes I am feeling healthy. Yes, I am still on these medicines. No, I have not thrown up or had any nausea recently. Yes, I have a good appetite. But will I make counts and do a round for the first time in almost a month? That is the real question.*

"Do you want me to count?"

I shrugged my shoulders and said, "Bring it on."

"One, two, three…"

The first stick actually pinched a little bit, something I wasn't expecting.

"Are you all right, Jonathan?"

"O yeah, I'm fine, just the first poke I've had in a while."

Like the first butterfly needle, the second stick stung a little bit, too. I grimaced for a split-second, and my mom and Rochelle did the same. Rochelle proceeded with the process of taking the blood from each side of the port. After about two minutes she crossed her fingers and smiled at me. She knew that I wasn't defensive about having to do chemo. I just wanted to attack each round head-on. Recently, my K-Life small group had brought up a sign one time that said, "ENTER WITH CAUTION: THIS IS THE ROOM OF DA CANCER KILLA." It made me laugh thinking back on it as Rochelle left the room.

Five minutes later, Rochelle walked in with a not-so-happy look on her face.

"Well I have some bad news."

"Uh oh, I didn't make counts…?"

"You have to do a round of Methotrexate," she said, her mouth instantly changing into a happy smile.

"I am *so* bummed," I said with a grin.

Bring it on.

The physical therapist came in a few hours later, and I probably worked harder in that session than ever before. Every day I experienced a range of emotions. I could be down in the dumps mentally one minute, and the next thing you know I could be pumping iron physically. It really didn't take much to make me feel better. Even if I wasn't feeling so hot, I tried to be nice and polite to everyone. One time I was on a week off, and my mom and I were eating at a restaurant. The waitress had served us before, but she noticed that I was bald and I had crutches. I could tell that she was curious by the way she looked at me when she asked me what I wanted to eat. My mom was going to the bathroom, and she took the chance that presented itself.

"My mom is a leukemia survivor," she said. "Do you mind my asking what kind of illness you have?"

"I have Osteogenic Sarcoma, a bone cancer."

"I guessed you had cancer because you are bald. I saw your scar, and it is so cool!"

I laughed and thanked her for that comment.

"How long did your mom go through treatment?" I asked.

"About two years," the waitress said. "It was really tough for my family but we stuck together. She is a fighter and she went through a lot to get where she is today. You guys are all amazing. I don't know what I would do if I had a diagnosis like that. How is your treatment going?"

"I was declared cancer-free on the day before my birthday, March 8," I told her.

"I am so happy for you! Do you have chemo left?"

"Yes I do, but it's easier to get through now that I know it has all been worth it. That makes all the difference."

"You seem to have a pretty good grip on your emotions. How old are you?"

"I am 18. I was diagnosed in November."

"Well good luck the rest of the way, kiddo," she said. "You don't need much help it sounds like!"

That statement had little truth to it, though, because I needed so much help along the way. A large portion of that support came from people who could lift my spirits up. I had lots of visitors. One of my favorites was Brooke, the Thursday night volunteer.

Love > Money

This world consists
Of material things
People work
Get paid
Wearing their diamond rings

To get by, to scrape by
Gotta pay those bills
Time is money
Money takes time
Using up hard work and skills

Assuming you have
A moment to spare
Helping others
Answers a prayer

With their hands tightly folded
And their heads bowed
The lost looked
To the heavens
And began praying out loud.

Doing good service
Will place joy in your heart
And bring more meaning
Than a paycheck
So volunteer for a start

On one particular night at the hospital in early May, I witnessed love like I hadn't seen before. Nick, a fellow patient on 4 Henson, was supposed to be getting a bone marrow transplant. Brooke had found out the week before from Nick's mom. They were ready to get it over with and Nick was so excited to put it behind him and move on. Unfortunately, the donor wasn't there on time. Brooke had stayed from 6:00 until about midnight, but when she found out about the delay, she decided to come back the next day at 5 p.m. She had a full time job editing a magazine, and yet she made sure she could be there with Nick and his family when he got his transplant. That is how much she cared about the patients. When people perform actions like that, the world is affected in such a positive way. She came into my room at 6:12 that night and gave me a big hug.

"Hey stinker, I haven't seen you in a while!"

I looked over at my mom and she knew that I wanted to talk to Brooke alone for a few minutes. She smiled and told me that she was just about to call dad and tell him that we had a room anyway.

Once I finished talking with my friend Brooke, she left and my nurse, Manda, came in. She gave me meds and then I fell asleep.

The next day was the Fourth of July, so the patriotic theme was visible all over the place. Blue and red was "paintballed" all over the floor. Linda Rix spent time with me again, and I was excited to be able to see fireworks from my bed. It was a huge blessing that the 4th was the only major holiday that I was missing.

At one point Linda took a call down the hall, and my nurse came in and introduced herself as Christina.

"I'm Jonathan, how are you?"

"I am a little stressed out tonight," she said. "Thanks for asking."

"Is it pretty busy?" I asked.

"Well, I just have three or four kiddos that are pretty high maintenance tonight." She said. "They all have meds to be hung so it is like being in several places at once."

She saw the shirt I was wearing, and it happened to be one of my youth group's mission trip shirts. It had a Bible verse on it and she told me that she had just read Job a few hours before she started work.

"I can't complain, especially after what you guys are going through on a daily basis," she said.

"It is natural for you to be upset about having a busy schedule," I told her. "Job is one of my favorite characters in the Bible, because he is stricken with hardships, and he remains faithful to God. I don't have it badly at all compared to some people."

We started talking and Linda came back in. I told the nurse I would be praying for her. I had told her that I was trying to write a book about this experience, and told her I would give her a copy once it was finished.

"Here is my email," she said. "Let me know when you are finished with it."

That night I knew. I knew that through God, maybe I could make a difference. I was undergoing treatment, which was not the most pleasant thing. But if I could take something difficult and be as positive and friendly as I could be, then maybe I could help others by attempting to emulate God's love. I finished this round on Sunday morning and left the hospital with a joyful heart. Just like a flower, when you plant a seed of faith, it's going to grow into something beautiful.

Chapter 23: Wisdom

Dedicated to: Phil Madden, former K-Life Leader

I am always amazed by how well some people know scripture in the Bible. My small group leader Phil is a true student of the Holy Word. I could probably ask him any question about a story in the Bible and use him as a reference. He is so wise for someone his age, and he can relate really well with younger people. I can talk to him about anything and feel comfortable, which is definitely not something that I can do with everyone. Listening is something that Phil is very adept at, and he always tries to look at things on both sides before offering advice. He has helped shape parts of my spiritual life, and I respect how he leads his life as a man of God.

Wisdom

For several months I had waited for this day. Everything had been prepared and I was waiting in eager anticipation. Times like this were special, and all I could do was *wait, wait, and wait.*

When we got to the clinic, Anna greeted us at the front desk. Out of the corner of my eye I saw Jamie through the door window that leads to the back part of the clinic. My heart started jumping because I was rarely the first person to get called back. Sure enough, when she came out she looked at me and said, "All right, Mr. Jonathan, we're ready for you."

"Are you just really excited to get chemo today or something?" she asked jokingly.

"Yep, that's it, you hit the nail right on the head…not!"

"So why are you really excited?" she asked.

"I only have four more rounds, so I am getting pretty close," I said. "Are you going up to the floor today?"

"Well yeah! I hear something cool is going on!" she said.

I nodded my head with a red face.

"I will try to leave the clinic for a few minutes so I can catch some of the celebration!"

Mary checked my breathing, asked if I was having any bathroom problems, and then told me we could go back to the big room to draw labs. As we were walking, she said, "Jonathan, I am so glad that you are off crutches and walking so well!"

"Thank you, it is weird to walk again, but I am sure getting used to it."

Mary went to get the labs ready, and I sat down next to my mom.

"The child-life specialist said that once you get admitted to the floor she will be up to help you."

"Hopefully it won't be too long," I said.

Mary came back with her tray-on-wheels and stuck both of the port sites. Once she finished she told me she would be back as soon as she got the results. Up until the point where she got back I prayed. God helped make that day one of the most memorable I have ever had when Mary came back with a thumbs-up. She showed me the results of my tests and said, "You're A-OK!"

I was truly overjoyed. Making counts was always something to be thankful for, but especially on this day.

I received fluids for hydration, and got to bed at 3:00. *This is good timing! I normally don't get up there this early!* Mom gave dad a call and let him know we were going up to the floor soon. Jamie escorted us up to the floor and she said that they would have a ceremony at 3:30. We rode up to the floor, and once Jamie scanned her card, we went through the double doors. Several nurses whistled and commented on my walking. I was so thankful to be off crutches and to make progress walking. Shanna was my nurse and she came in and asked me if something special was going on today. Dad came in and Shanna said, "I am confused because your son is being sneaky! Something special is going on today, but he won't tell me what!"

Amanda, the head of Child Life, popped her head into the room and told me she was ready. The floor speaker sounded, "Would all available nurses please proceed to the Child Life room? Would all available nurses please proceed to the Child Life room? Thank you."

In the Child Life room Amanda got up in front of all the nurses and the other staff in the room and told them about the fundraiser. I can't recall everything she said, but I remember everyone in the room. The "Bracketology for Oncology" fundraiser was a surprise to everyone. Amanda said, "Jonathan, will you do the honors and show them how much you raised?"

I slowly lifted the check and the nurses got very excited.

"Jonathan's supporters raised $4,400 for the floor, which allowed us to purchase a new coffee machine for the nurses," Amanda announced. "We will also be supplying boxes filled with different kinds of coffee! A local celebrity had donated money so that every room on the floor and in the clinic could have Nintendo Wii's. With this fundraiser, every room will also get two controllers and a numchuck! We also have game points so we can purchase Wii games in the future! The remaining donation money was used to purchase universal remotes for the floor and to make a contribution to the Nursing Scholarship fund."

Amanda told everyone to look to their left, and everyone cheered even more. Now it was my turn to be surprised. Sitting on the table were the controllers and numchucks. Stacked in rows, you couldn't even see the table there anymore.

"We cleared the shelves at four Target stores and they gave us a little discount when they heard what we were buying them for," Amanda said.

Nicole, the nice young lady who had helped coordinate everything, lined everyone up and we took a picture. We gave each other hugs.

"Dude, I didn't know about this!" Mandy said. "Seriously, Jonathan, that is so awesome, all of the patients are really going to appreciate that. Not to mention we are all going to love the coffee machine," she said with a laugh.

There were cookies for everyone and some of the nurses started trying out the new coffee machine.

"I know there's a lot of coffee in those boxes, but I wouldn't count on it lasting very long," Amy said with a smile. "We have some serious java addicts on this floor."

After a few more minutes, the room started clearing out a little and I watched the child life workers clear off the table so they could hide the Wii controllers. I thanked Amanda for helping me and she gave me a hug and thanked me. But it wasn't me who needed to be thanked; it was the people who contributed to the cause. Anybody can think of an idea for a fundraiser, but it is not going to work unless people care enough to give to it. When I got back in to my room, I thought of how much my view on giving and receiving had changed. What you possess can be taken away. Need equals necessity, want equals desire. It is such a privilege to give. That weekend was the fastest I had ever excreted Methotrexate, and I left with a big smile on my face.

Chapter 24: XXIV

Dedicated to: Dr. Howard Rosenthal, my Orthopedic Surgeon

If you ever have any questions regarding knee joints, the first person I could direct you to would be a surgeon by the name of Dr. Howard Rosenthal. Now serving as my primary physician, Dr. Rosenthal was the surgeon who performed the knee replacement surgery. Other than the fact that he is an extremely gifted surgeon, he has a personality that gives a sense of calm in the midst of a storm. I cannot count how many visits I have had at his office for check-ups, and every time I've had the chance to talk with him, he is eager to know how my life is going. Who knows how many times I will visit him over the course of my life, but I look forward to talking with him each time. My visits up to his office do not seem like check-ups anymore, just getting re-acquainted with an old friend. Thank you Dr. Rosenthal, and thank you to Kim and Melissa for being such great nurses.

CAMPIONS

XXIV

In a way, having cancer treatment is a lot like running a marathon. At the starting line, you might be a little nervous for the gunshot to begin the race. Once your blood starts pumping, you are off. Setting a steady pace is not easy at the beginning, but eventually you build speed and develop a rhythm. The first several rounds are by far the toughest, but you have to keep in mind that you have 14 or 15 rounds left to go. There is no stopping and walking; you have trained too hard.

There are times when you will get chemo three weekends in a row, and you don't have much time to recover in between the Sunday you leave the hospital and the Thursday when you come back. You are halfway through the race and you are starting to feel the fatigue set in. Chemo becomes easier because you are starting to figure out what works best to keep nausea down. The mouth sores are more bearable, but it is still difficult to eat. Time goes faster until you realize you are a couple of miles away from the finish line.

It is surreal how fast the race has gone by. You are only a couple of weeks away from the light at the end of the tunnel. The end of the race is in sight and your body is worn down. Chemotherapy is almost finished so you are counting down the days you have left. Before you know it, you sprint through the tape at the finish line. You did it! You beat cancer and the prognosis is excellent!

Nine months ago you started a journey, and 18 rounds of chemotherapy later, you are cancer-free. So many people are affected by cancer, it is hard to accept that even some of the toughest die fighting. Some of the sweetest kids I met didn't get to finish their treatment, but they tried their best.

There are first and last times for everything in life, and I was about to experience one of those "lasts," God willing. The red chemotherapy I had gotten, Doxorubicin, was on its final leg. All it would take was a final two-day infusion, and barring any setbacks I could then go home with two out of the three different kinds of chemo completed. This medicine was the least likely to cause nausea. Walking into the clinic, waiting in a chair, I was thinking: *This round shouldn't be bad at all. It was fine last time so it should be a piece of cake, right?*

Ironically enough, it was a rough weekend. The start was not bad, as I was rested and ready for this round. The clinic wait was not shorter than usual, but it felt like it was. I talked to David off and on, and also to Shelley. Jamie was now working more up on the floor in the Infusion Room, so she would only be in the clinic one or two days a week. Kaylynne was finished in the clinic, because she was on another floor working as a care assistant. Talking with these friends made me realize how nice it was to see a familiar face every time you came to clinic.

Almost

When you've been counting forever
Eternally longing, it seems
It's like waiting for teakettles
To boil and steam

You know the end's coming
Although when it gets here
You'll be utterly amazed
At how you've overcome your fear

The scare is long over
Just a moment remains
You'd give anything to be finished
You will never be the same

This time has been taxing
The most taxing thus far
But you can't hold frustration
All cooped up in a jar

If and if only
There is a will and a way
After three more rounds of treatment
You can call it a day

My life after completing chemotherapy would change dramatically. This is something that I didn't want to think about. I just sat and closed my eyes in the large room of our clinic and tried to rest. This plan failed miserably. Rochelle came over and the minute I heard her voice I knew immediately what to do. Before I heard words form I pointed in the general direction of the bathroom and said, "Urine sample?"

"Yes sir, you are sharp as a tack," she answered with a grin.

I kind of felt like a robot once Rochelle came back and started to poke me because I had been through this routine so many times. It didn't hurt when she stuck the ports and she began checking blood flow. Both sides were working A-OK so she proceeded to draw my blood. After about 45 minutes, I got the answer I was waiting for.

"You're all clear, Mr. Jonathan!" Rochelle said. "I will bring your chemo as soon as Nancy gives you an evaluation."

"Wow, so you'll be done with this drug after this weekend, right?" mom asked.

"Yeah, and then just two more rounds altogether," I said with a happy look.

My mom looked like she had seen the prettiest sunrise. I realized that my parents' lives would also change when I finished all of the chemo. They wouldn't be recovering from the medicine, but they had sacrificed more than I will ever realize. They no longer would need to go to the hospital with me to stay when I got admitted, and a new chapter of their lives would begin. Nancy and I went to an exam room and she asked me the questions. None of my medication had changed. I was eating and drinking all right at the moment, and the mouth sores were too bad. I was trying to take care of myself and to use good oral hygiene. I was so blessed because a friend of dad, who is an adult cancer specialist, recommended a liquid that helped so much with the mouth sores. This was an answered prayer!

"Are you getting excited that you are reaching the end?"

"So excited," I said in a quiet joyful voice.

In the main room of the clinic, Rochelle brought the pre-chemo meds and I instantly downed them with water. Almost an hour later, she brought in the chemo and programmed the infusion to begin. Hours passed and I had frequent visits by Shelley and David. Occasionally they would bring snacks like chips or Lorna Doone cookies, but I would mainly just tell them I was doing OK.

The round started with the potential to be the shortest visit yet. Brooke came and talked to me and I put the oil on my scar. No longer resembling a shark bite, it was starting to disappear a little bit. Over time it would fade more and more. It was, however, an everlasting mark. It was the symbol that would be a daily reminder of how lucky I had been with the treatment from November 2007 to August 2008 — and beyond.

Shark Bite

No, a shark never bit me
Although how interesting that would be
Some people say a story
Is what they will look and see

The only fable living
Is my journey under the knife
The one thing that took six hours
And prolonged my complacent life

This test of faith
Of courage bold
When these pages are finished
Is a story I will have told

I can only hope
That people know
God's the only reason
My spirit did not stay low

With God's help I had persevered thus far. Friday came along and things went swimmingly. The infusion continued and on Friday afternoon the 24-hour mark passed. *Only one more day and I get to go home.* That night my mom came back to the hospital after I had been with my dad all day. My mouth was fine and I didn't have any nausea. Andrea was my nurse for the next two nights and I was so glad. She was very sweet and always fun to talk to. That night after she came in and took my vitals she told me she was going to check in on other patients. I dozed off after she asked if I needed anything. I woke up in the middle of the night and the clock read 2:45. Rarely had I just passed out like that for almost eight hours. I didn't sit up; I just looked around the pitch-blackness until my eyes adjusted. The curtain was closed and so was the door to my room. I was looking over to where my mom was sleeping and heard a noise. It was the sound of the door slowly creaking and Andrea tip-toeing in after pulling the curtain open a little bit. I almost laughed at how stealthily she was moving. When she pressed one of the buttons on the IV pump, I turned my head and whispered, *"Andrea."*

She jumped and let out a deep sigh when she saw my smiling face looking at her. She didn't want to wake up my mom, so she told me she would talk to me the next night.

The next evening I was about an hour away from finishing the infusion, and I hiccupped. *Uh...oh...* I thought. That was a bad sign, because the last time I had hiccups, they lasted for two hours. Reglan was ordered, but it had not arrived. The worst part was that my parents were both out doing errands. I dry-heaved. Sometimes this is worse than actually throwing up because when you throw up you feel better. I got up and walked around, and I tried going to the bathroom, but neither worked. I told my parents I wasn't feeling well and that I was hiccupping. When they arrived, a dose of Reglan was delivered, and my nurse gave it to me. It worked for about 20 minutes, but then the hiccups came back. My stomach started hurting, and Andrea came in to give more Reglan. I was praying and praying. Andrea told me that the drug would start kicking in, and she was right. After that dose I was finished with the hiccups and dry heaving. My prayers had been answered, and we didn't care that I had to spend the night and go home the next morning.

Chapter 25: Youth Group

Dedicated to: Kyle Gardner, Youth Pastor

One of the first people I told about my diagnosis was my youth pastor. The first thing he said was, "If anyone can handle this and make it through, it is you."

The youth group had a head-shaving party in support of me. One of the youth members designed do-rags that said "Stepping Together" written in gold. Five out of the nine months that I have been getting treatment, Kyle shaved his head. The youth group had been close to me throughout high school, but when I was diagnosed, they became a second family. There is not one person in the group that I would feel uncomfortable talking to. Kyle has been with me through it all. I cannot imagine how amazing of a dad he will be. He is a father figure for several kids in our youth group, as well as having his own. Thank you, Kyle, and your wife, Sara.

Braving Discipleship
2007

Youth Group

Cisplatin? Check! Doxorubicin? I just crossed that one off, too. I still have two rounds of Methotrexate left... That didn't make me worry, but it did make me long for everything to be over. I don't think I had ever wanted to speed up time as much as I did right now. I was on my break because there had been three rounds of chemo in a row. I felt a little weak but I didn't feel like I would collapse. I was, as always, happy to be home, but to be at the hospital the next two weekends would have been OK with me. I enjoyed the warm weather, but often got too warm when I was outside. I had been to a couple of graduation parties earlier in the summer, and I learned that I needed to keep cool. In the hospital I usually wanted the room to be colder because I liked being able to shed layers if I had a fever. The time off was going well— until I woke up sweating in the middle of the night before I was scheduled to do my next round of chemo. My temperature was 101.3° and dad and I headed for the hospital.

"Are you nauseated?"

"No, just really hot."

"I hate to bring this up, but when you had mucositis and we went to the Emergency Room, you were in a wheelchair, and you threw up as we went through the door," my dad said.

We both were thankful for how far I had come. This would only be the third time going through the ER and to me that wasn't that bad. It was about 11:00 at night, so the only way I could be admitted was through the Emergency Room. Before this whole experience I had always the ER being this horrible place you never wanted to be in. I found out that you obviously didn't want to be there unless something went very wrong, but it was not a bad environment. The correct term would be "intense." Before you were admitted, they listened to your history and checked you out. Thankfully, this particular time, the ER was short. My floor had a bed open because someone had just been discharged. *This is definitely a blessing.*

"Mr. Jonathan, I'm confused. Why did you come in to see us early? Did you just miss us that badly?" one of the nurses joked.

Dad told me he was going to call my mom and tell her that I was in a room. A new nurse named Monika, supervised by Emily, pulled out the butterfly needles to access the port.

Both sides were working fine, and she drew blood to check for infection.

My mom came in later that night and my dad headed home. Monika and Emily came in to check on me periodically throughout the night. I learned quickly that Monika would be a great addition to the floor taking care of kids. She was very kind and every time I saw her from then on, I had a special connection with her. I had been one of the first kids she had taken care of. Emily told me teenagers were the best to use as "guinea pigs" because they usually cooperate.

Another nurse going through orientation on the floor was named Jenny. She was on day shift and even though she started orienting toward the end of my treatment, she had a personality that made it feel like we were old friends. She was a KU grad and was really funny to talk to. She could joke around but she also had a sweet side. The great thing about 4 Henson is that every single person who works there cares about their job.

Everyone has days when things aren't going so hot, but they still work hard because they know people's lives are in their hands. They took such good care of me. I felt at ease because I had so much faith and trust in that floor's staff.

I was in the hospital until Sunday, but by then I was feeling much better! I had no fever for 48 hours. I talked with my parents and we decided that it would be a good idea to go ahead and do the next round of chemo that Thursday. Those next four days went by pretty slowly. Finally Thursday arrived, and I was so relieved.

When we returned to the clinic, Rochelle drew the labs and after 40 minutes she came back and told me that everything was all clear. I had missed a call, so I listened to my voicemail. It was from Kyle, and he told me that everyone was praying for me like crazy. He said that he wanted to see me soon, and so did all the youth group.

This message from Kyle was what I needed. Nobody could have made me feel better at the moment than he could. Knowing my youth group supported me made me think, *Be strong for them. Get out of here knowing you finished strong.* That weekend treatment went very well, and I had a renewed sense of endurance and strength. Why do something if you're not going to do it to the fullest? The road was long and there were many obstacles, but now was not the time to finish. Round 18 was about to start, and I was ready for this moment.

Chapter 26: Zion

Dedicated to: Albro Stepp & Weldon Crank, my grandfathers

Have you ever thought about how beautiful our world is? We sometimes take our environment for granted so it is easy to forget about its natural splendor. If Earth is so beautiful, how much more majestic will heaven be? Who can possibly imagine. . . but when I get to heaven I will be reunited with one of my grandfathers, and will meet one of them for the first time. My parents named me Jonathan because it means "Gift of God". My middle name, Albro, was my grandfather's name. My two grandfathers were very different. One was a banker from Kansas City, and the other was an engineer from Dallas. What they had in common was their generosity and loving nature. We all had cancer, and unfortunately, lung cancer took Albro a few months after I was born, while it took Weldon's life five Thanksgivings ago. When I was diagnosed I wondered if I would be seeing them soon. I told myself that it wasn't time, and I put on the boxing gloves. A day before my birthday in March, I received the news that the bone from my operation was 100% cancer-free. My grandfathers led wonderful lives, and I miss them dearly.

Zion

"7:45" the clock read.

Excitement (adj.): 1. The feeling of lively and cheerful joy; 2. The state of being emotionally aroused and worked up.

You could take that definition and multiply it times one hundred, and not even scratch the surface of how I was feeling. If there was a Cloud Nine, then I was on Cloud Ten. There are peaks in life, and there are valleys, and I had experienced each. I spent months thinking about the prospect of what was about to happen. There was so much emotion, and so much energy that I cannot put it into words.

The time was now 7:46 a.m. I sat in bed and chuckled to myself. *Wow, I need to calm down.*

After a quick shower and a terrible packing job, I practically sprinted to the garage. Mom couldn't get in the car any faster. They sensed my excitement, too.

"You are ready, aren't you?" they asked.

"Yeah, just a little bit," I said jokingly.

We can get the streamers and party favors out when I make counts.

We took the route to the hospital deemed to be the fastest (who knew if it actually was, but then again, I didn't really care!). The clock read 8:04. We got closer with each stoplight, and I swear I could've jumped out of the car. A police car sped past on one of the streets, and I secretly desired to hitch a ride with it and bypass all of the traffic. We got to 31st and Gillham

Road and I knew that we were close to our destination. We pulled into the front entrance, veered left, and made our way down into the depths of the parking garage. mom pulled in and once she shifted gears I pulled the door handle and it slowly opened. I stepped out of the mini-van and started walking.

"I'm going to go check in at the clinic," I said.

Once in the elevator, I headed up to the hospital lobby and walked to the next elevator that would take me to 2nd floor. Soon I walked across the hall and entered the Hem/Onc Clinic through the heavy wooden door.

"This is it, isn't it?" said Anna, as I walked up to the desk.

"Yes," I said. "The last one."

The Exodus

Until the day comes
You might never know
Just how good it feels
To conquer this foe

The days, the hours,
The minutes you waited
Weren't as long as those ticking seconds
That cannot be debated

It happened so fast
When I found it in scans
Now everything will be over
That was part of God's plan

It seemed like forever
But it was only a fraction
You've gained more in that year
Than in 18 of previous action

There were forces above
Helping you make it through
Soon your story's a memory
Others can find faith in too.

Shelley walked out of the door that led back to the clinic with a smile on her face.

"Hello bud, we are ready for you."

I couldn't help but smile as I followed her back to the height/weight room for what was hopefully my last time as a patient. The clock on the wall now said 8:24, and I was sitting down on the bench taking off my shoes. Shelley put the medium-sized blood pressure cuff on my left arm as I took the thermometer and placed it in the back of my throat. My blood pressure was fairly high, so Shelley asked if we could take it again after learning my temperature was fine. I told her we could take it five more times but I would still be excited. After we found a more reasonable result, we chuckled and decided that it wasn't going to get any better.

Mom popped her head in the door and told me she would be in the big room in the back. I soon followed her lead and Shelley escorted us into an examining room. Once inside Nancy checked my vitals and Rochelle came in with IV fluids. She wiped off the port site and used the cleaning swab to sterilize it. Once she did that she asked if I wanted her to count before she stuck me. I used my patented response and told her that it was fine either way but she counted anyway. One was in, and thirty seconds later the other butterfly needle was too. I had one desire, and that one desire was to make counts. Once that happened, everything would be perfect (or as close as you can get to that word). Dr. Shore came up and congratulated me.

"Well it wasn't always easy, but you my friend, are nearly finished," he said.

"I still remember when I met you last November," I told him with a smile.

"I remember when I met you too, and that seems like forever ago."

Nancy commented on how far I had come, and she told me how proud she was of me. I wanted to start crying, but I had gotten good at holding it in.

"Once we get your counts back, we will try to get you up there as soon as we can," Dr. Shore said. "Do you need anything?"

"Just to make counts," I answered. "Otherwise I'm all set."

"I hear you might be having some type of celebration later?" he asked.

"I don't know about that," I said with a stifled laugh.

"We will try to make it by when that starts," Nancy said with a wink.

I ended up waiting for the lab results while listening to pump-up music. I looked at the clock and fifteen minutes had gone by. I double-checked and was amazed at how fast that quarter of an hour had gone by. I pressed "play" again on the iPod and felt a tap on my knee that startled me. It felt weird, so I looked up quickly to see who it was. Surely enough, the redheaded nurse that had taken care of me so many times in clinic was leaning over me, and she whispered something with a straight face.

"You made it."

That straight face instantly changed into a smile and I choked because I laughed so excitedly. As if I had just been shocked by a spark plug, my body began feeling all fidgety and restless. My mom was the first one to hear the good news besides me, and she gave Rochelle a big hug. Nothing could repay her, or any of the staff at Children's Mercy. The conclusion of chemotherapy was rapidly approaching.

One of the Child Life workers came into the clinic and approached me as I was getting up to take a stroll.

"Hey, Jonathan! We wanted to know if you wanted chocolate or vanilla cake, and if you wanted sprinkles on it or not?"

After over nine months of tough decisions, it was a relief to make one that was so easy.

"Alrighty, hopefully we'll see you soon!" she said.

As I waited to get a bed up on the floor, several people tell me how excited they were for me to be finished with treatment. By the time they were ready up on the floor, I was literally pacing around. I gave some of the nurses in the clinic hugs, and Rochelle wished me good luck for the weekend.

I thanked her, and after getting on the elevator, I let out a big sigh of relief.

"Thank you for letting me make counts," I prayed under my breath as we got off the elevator and walked down to the Sutherland/Henson Towers.

My mom had called my dad so he and my brother Nathan came up right behind us on the elevator. We went in with Shelley and pressed the round "4" button that would take me up to do the last round of chemo I would ever receive. My mom patted me on the back as we waited silently for Shelley to swipe her keycard to get on the floor.

This weekend did not feel the same as all the others, because it felt like it was all a going away party. Everyone I saw either shook my hand or gave me a hug and words of congratulations (or both).

My brother and my dad came into the hallway as I was heading to the Child Life Room. Everyone had been telling me that a curly-haired kid my height was walking around with my dad, and I instantly knew who they were talking about. I gave him a hug that brothers give and he said, “Man, you just keep growing!”

“Actually, I am finished growing. I think I am just taller than you,” I said in a smart-aleck manner.

The ceremony/party for the last round of chemo was heartfelt. Child Life presented me with a Target gift card and a full barrage of Axe products (i.e. body wash, hair gel, deodorant, etc.) We had cake and several of the toddler patients and their families came. Manda stopped by and told me congratulations. That night, Brooke came at 6 and brought me a card as well. For this special occasion, I chose to have KFC delivered by my dad, and Brooke and I split it. She gave me several big hugs, and kisses on the cheek. She would be my life-long friend.

That night I had Andrea and I got the chance to talk to her about life and thank her for her help and friendship. The next day I was so happy to learn that the Methotrexate level was low, and that Mandy was my nurse. I had been looking forward to Saturday, and was excited to see many nurses and care assistants that I hadn’t seen in a while. My mom brought French Silk pie up the floor, and towards the evening, Matt (my psychologist, who was really my fellow sports nut) came in with a very meaningful card and we chatted. Another lifelong friend.

Around six o'clock I invited Mandy into my room with April, and we had pie together. I gave them each a card and thanked them. The week before this final chemo I had decided to write one for every person that had taken care of me. Mandy stayed after April said goodbye, and she gave me a card from the nurses, and a card from her. I started crying and I stopped myself because she said, "We can both cry tomorrow! You are making me cry!"

Mandy was yet another special friend who I will always cherish.

Andrea came into my room that night and I gave her my card when she changed the fluids. She started tearing up and she stayed in the room and talked for a few minutes. The night before all the nurses had ordered food from Minsky's and Andrea had ordered me a meatball sub even though I was already stuffed. She had been so nice to me, and I will always remember her kindness during one of the roughest nights at the hospital (I think she changed the bed sheets five times). I said goodbye to her in the middle of the night and she gave me a big hug.

The next morning, I woke up with mixed feelings; Andrea had left me a note saying the Methotrexate level was low enough to go home. We waited until noon to get un-hooked because Leslie and her husband brought their adorable baby daughter to the floor for us to see. Mandy did the honors of taking the needles out and I felt a surge of freedom. No more chemotherapy. No more seeing my second family on a regular basis. I knew there would be calls. Texts. Hugs. I also knew that both of my grandfathers and would be looking down proudly. Mom once told me that the day I was born, my Papa got diagnosed. I never knew him, but I loved him. This victory was for him. It was for my Granddad. After the good-byes, mom and I went downstairs, escorted by Mandy. By the car, I thanked Mandy and I began to cry.

Tears of Sadness, Tears of Joy

As I had leaped
From the Arctic Pole
To the Equator
A waterfall plunged down my cheeks

My dream was no longer
Just a figment of sleep
It was something emerging
From the mind's valleys; so deep

I saw Everest's peaks
And God willing I knew
That I would not have gotten anywhere
Without someone like you.

As we drove away, I thought of the pigeons in the windows, pecking and strutting— and flying! The hospital on the hill faded. I beamed with brightness as tears rolled down my eyes. God helped me to be a fighter and He is the reason I won. Amen.

Song of Joy

I write from my heart,
Singing and writing of joy as each tomorrow greets me.

My knee, every tendon replaced, met with metal, with strength,
Every obstacle faced, God has faced and conquered,
Cancer, now absent from the depths of my being,
Launching me forward into thankful living.
I cannot complain forevermore, I would be banished from my own existence,
To breathe with humility,
With Christ's mercy.

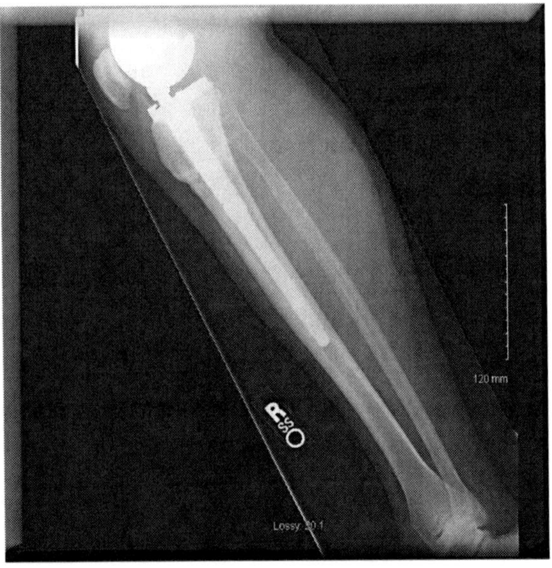

Words Cannot Express Everything I Wish I Could Say

Where would I be if I did not have the support of my family, friends, and even those I don't know? This story thanks a lot of individuals specifically, but it does not come close to truly thanking everyone that is responsible for helping me and lifting me up during tough times. I truly wish I could include everyone that has been there for me in this book, but it is not possible. There are names upon names of people who were there for me. Whether it was by cooking a meal, volunteering to spend time with me to give my parents a night off, giving a generous gift, or through the gift of time, I will never truly grasp how impactful the power of support is. I would like to take this opportunity to reach out and thank each and every one of the families, nurses, doctors, and individuals who took it upon themselves to be a rock in my life. I *truly* could not have done it without you, and I will never forget how much you showered me with love, kindness, and selfless acts of generosity. My heart goes out to all of you. On behalf of both my family, and myself, I extend a huge thank you for your care and compassion.

Medical Glossary (Don't worry if this means nothing to you. It's mainly to make some kind of sense of what I'm talking about when it comes to the drugs I was given for treatment, and the medical jib-jab associated with it all.)

ANC - Absolute neutrophil count; calculated from regular blood count and used to determine risk of infection.

Lorazepam *(Ativan)* - A drug that is given to prevent nausea and vomiting during chemotherapy. I took this drug once.

Cisplatin - One of three chemo drugs administered to me… An anti-cancer, a clear-colored drug that was the most intense one used during my treatment.

Dexamethasone *(Decadron)* - A steroid used to help prevent nausea and vomiting.

Doxorubicin - One of three chemo drugs administered to me… Another "anti-cancer", a red colored drug that caused hair loss, can affect heart function, and causes fatigue (some of the side effects)

Aprepitant *(Emend)* - The "miracle" drug that helped keep me from having nausea and vomiting, literally the most helpful drug I have ever taken.

Granisetron *(Kytril)* - A drug used to prevent nausea and vomiting.

Marinol - An appetite stimulant that is an alternative to "medicinal marijuana", causes same "high feeling" while helping prevent nausea and vomiting. I did not take this drug long…

Methotrexate - The chemo drug that I had for 12 out of the 18 rounds at Children's Mercy. An "anti-cancer", a neon yellow drug that caused bad mouth sores, loss of appetite, and vomiting and nausea.

Mucositis - The formation of mouth sores all along the G.I. tract as a result from different chemotherapy drugs (mainly Methotrexate in my case).

Neutropenic Fever *(or Neutropenia)* - Low white blood cells/ neutrophils from chemotherapy, and my body could not fight off a fever. This frequently is a cause for hospitalization

Nystatin - Used to help prevent and soothe mouth sores induced by chemotherapy.

Osteogenic Sarcoma - (My) cancer of the bone that commonly affects the large bones of the arm or leg (in my case the right tibia).

Oxycodone - A strong painkiller that was used during chemotherapy and after total knee surgery.

Oxycontin - Another pain reliever commonly used.

Promethazine *(Phenergan)* - A drug used to prevent nausea and vomiting.

Port-a-cath - A small medical appliance that was installed beneath my left collarbone that allowed me to receive medicine, chemotherapy, and fluids intravenously (with an IV). One surgery to install this saved me hundreds of pokes in my arms...

Metoclopramide *(Reglan)* - A drug used to help prevent nausea and vomiting, also used to prevent intense hiccups (no, I am not kidding).

Ondansetron *(Zofran)* - Another drug to help with nausea and vomiting.

CPSIA information can be obtained at www.ICGtesting.com
Printed in the USA
LVOW07s0406101014

408035LV00002B/2/P

9 781449 783990